D0443358

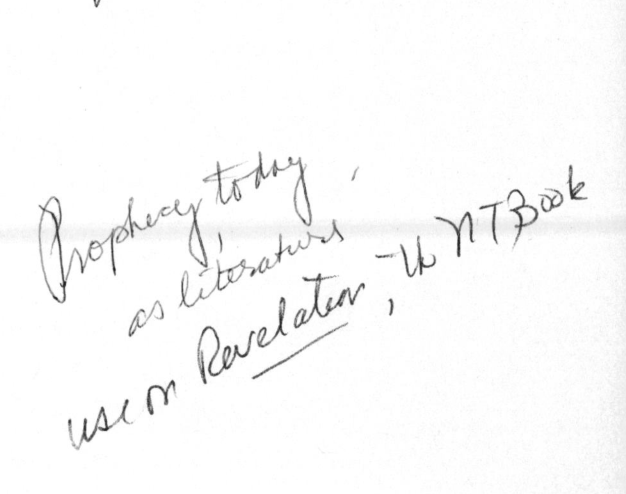
Prophecy today
as literature
use in Revelation, the NT Book

THE RECOVERY
OF CHRISTIAN MYTH

The Recovery of Christian Myth

by

GUILFORD DUDLEY III

THE WESTMINSTER PRESS
Philadelphia

1967

Grateful acknowledgment is made to:

Alfred A. Knopf, Inc., for quotations from *Doctor Faustus: The Life of the German Composer Adrian Leverkühn as Told by a Friend,* by Thomas Mann, translated by H. T. Lowe-Porter. Copyright 1948 by Alfred A. Knopf, Inc.
Doubleday & Company, Inc., for quotations from *The Sot-Weed Factor,* by John Barth. Copyright © 1960 by John Barth.
J. B. Lippincott Company, for quotations from *The Crying of Lot 49,* by Thomas Pynchon; copyright 1966.
McGraw-Hill Book Company, Inc., for quotations from *Billiards at Half-past Nine,* by Heinrich Böll. Copyright © 1962 by Kiepenheuer & Witsch.
New Directions Publishing Corporation, for quotations from *Miss Lonelyhearts* and *Day of the Locust,* by Nathanael West. Copyright 1933 by Nathanael West; 1960 by Laura S. Perelman.
Random House, Inc., for quotations from *The Possessed,* by Fyodor Dostoyevsky (Avrahm Yarmolinsky, translator); copyright 1936 and renewed 1963 by Random House, Inc.; and for quotations from *Invisible Man,* by Ralph Ellison; copyright 1947, 1948, 1952, by Ralph Ellison.
The Viking Press, Inc., for quotations from *Women in Love,* by D. H. Lawrence. Copyright 1920, 1922, by D. H. Lawrence; 1948, 1950, by Frieda Lawrence.

Library of Congress Catalog Card No. 67–15869

Published by The Westminster Press ®
Philadelphia, Pennsylvania

PRINTED IN THE UNITED STATES OF AMERICA

To my wife and son:
Elizabeth and Christen

I John, your brother, who share with you in Jesus the tribulation and the kingdom and the patient endurance, was on the island called Patmos on account of the word of God and the testimony of Jesus.

—*The Revelation to John 1:9*

CONTENTS

ACKNOWLEDGMENTS

MY DEBT to others for the privilege of calling this my book is one I feel unable to discharge in writing. Each time I read these pages, it becomes clearer in what a limited sense I am their author. They contain the inspiration, the thoughts, and inevitably the words of teachers and friends. In addition to the books acknowledged in the notes, I am immensely grateful to four people. Paul S. Minear has helped me to see both the significance and the meaning of the book of Revelation, and it was through his inspiration and encouragement that this project got under way. R. W. B. Lewis first brought my attention to the apocalyptic imagination in modern fiction through a seminar at Yale sponsored by Dwight Hall, and his graduate seminar in English helped reveal this dimension in Lawrence, Dostoevsky, and Mann. David B. Harned, Associate Professor of Religion at Smith College, has devoted a summer to reading revisions of the manuscript, a contribution that should be cited for its sheer generosity as well as for its critical value. My final debt of gratitude is to my wife, who both encouraged and endured me through it all.

GUILFORD DUDLEY III

Stamford, Connecticut

Moderns churchmen are embarrassed by myth

INTRODUCTION

A LEADING figure in American Protestantism has frequently told the press: "With the decline of Christianity, it is necessary to travel light. I want to get rid of as much theological baggage as I can."[1] That laconic remark typifies an attitude that is growing among Protestant churches in this country. In their zeal to arrest the so-called decline of Christianity, the churches are showing an alarming readiness to jettison all concepts and language that do not immediately conform to what they have judged to be the canons of modernity. The language they have abandoned most willingly and with least discrimination is symbol and myth. This decision has put them on a perilous course, leaving them adrift and even farther removed from genuine communication with our culture. They are misassessing the culture, and limiting both the meaning of modernity and the language of the gospel.

This book is a study of how much is at stake in the very mythic language which the churches are hastening to disown, and indeed how hard that language dies in the heart of our famished culture. For even though mythic language seems to have been banished from the official parlance of the church, it has reappeared in major works of literary art that give testimony to its vivifying power. The churches have consigned to near oblivion the book of Revelation, the most stubbornly mythic book in the New Testament canon; yet a growing literary tradition of the apocalyptic imagination in fiction is restoring the myth to a living part of our cultural heritage. The great Christian myth of the Apocalypse is enjoying a remarkable exile.

In point of fact, our American culture is mythic to the core. We feed upon paltry myths that delude and betray us, leaving us the victims of famine which only a myth with the staple of truth can relieve. Contrary to the judgment of the churches, the world's coming of age has not destroyed the primal search for truth which yearns for integrating rather than atomizing vision, nor has it quenched the longing for communion with epic figures in a cosmic drama. Where the Christian churches refuse to provide the picture and the drama, we turn to the culture for substitute myths but find none that fully satisfies, and the artist mirrors our dilemma. In the artist's mirror, the futility of our time appears against the backdrop of a myth whose scope is immense and awesome. To the hungering among us he offers to rejuvenate a mythic consciousness, and the myth of which he makes us acutely aware is that of the Apocalypse. Now that the artist has shown us its foreboding darkness, the Christian churches are left with the task of seeing and proclaiming the light that once dawned so majestically upon those who shared its vision. Whether the churches will affirm the redemptive myth as a Word to heal and transfigure our culture depends upon two questions: whether they can perceive its relevance and whether they still recognize intrinsic value in their native language of symbol and myth.

That language has intrinsic worth because only the roads of symbolic and mythic speech provide access to the faith perspective of those who testified to the crucifixion-resurrection event which is the foundation of Christianity. That is to say, the substance of the gospel is embedded in a mythic or archetypal consciousness. That consciousness can be entered only on its own terms. The event that set the course of the Easter faith burned into the minds of the apostolic writers a network of analogies extending into time and space. When the crucified One rose, God did something new. "All things new" (*panta kaina*) became a shout of joy (Rev. 21:5); with their awesome fanfare, the heavenly trumpets announced nothing less than a new cosmic situation, a "new creation." That is why the theologian uses the word "ontological"; it is why the literary critic uses the word "mythological." The two are inseparable; a new world like this cannot be wrenched from the story in which it is embedded without loss. Historical criticism has an important function, but its work is always tentative: the critic can never divorce the theological content from its linguistic form. Amos Wilder has rightly observed that "the transposition of myth into provisional discursive or existential analogies is desirable provided it be recognized that every such formulation is a poor surrogate and must always again appeal back to the original. . . . The language of the New Testament has a large part of imaginative rhetoric, alone adequate to catch up the awareness and world-sense of the believers. The only way we can really understand it and communicate it is to enter into its original power."[2]

To say that a mythic consciousness is necessary to appreciate or understand the resurrection is not to imply a denial of its historicity. But it is to say that as a historical event the Easter event compelled its witnesses to envision the horizons of time and space into which it reached. The book of Revelation gives expression to these dimensions as no other book in the New Testament. In this sense it contains the beginnings of the new language of the gospel: there we can observe the birth-pangs of a new Word/world perspective which lies in the background of all other writings in the New Testament. John wrote what he saw and heard in the cosmic extension of the crucifixion-resurrection victory:

> Fear not, I am the first and the last, and the living one; I died, and behold I am alive for evermore, and I have the keys of Death and Hades. Now write what you see. (Rev. 1:17–19.)

He sees the extension of the historical event in the imagery that dominates the vision. The presiding image is the regnant Lamb, the exaltation of him who was sacrificed. But he does not rule, nor is he exalted in isolation from the community of the redeemed. To share John's vision is to see the one King and the many kings as characters in a cosmic drama. Other related images give mythic expression to the death-resurrection event: the crown, the throne, the book of life, the tree of life, the open door, the new name, the new song, the new city, the new creation, the trumpets, the sound of many waters, and the white robes. These form a network of images through which the Lamb's victory manifests itself. They present a cosmology of time and space that gives the victory the fullest orbit which the language of the gospel can offer.

The first part of this essay deals with the degree to which the churches have banished myth from their language and consciousness, and with the treasure of which they are depriving themselves and their mission. In Part Two the focus shifts to the power of the myth in exile, now being resuscitated by the novelist and absorbed by the very reading public that the churches have stereotyped as doggedly opposed to mythic language.

PART ONE
MYTH AND THE CHURCH

1

RETREAT FROM THE MYTHICAL

A technological society is a society of disenchantment.
—James M. Gustafson.

UNTIL the scientific revolution it was generally acknowledged that man could not live without myths in which he could believe, with which he could identify, and through which he could communicate. Myth gave expression to the vibrant mystery of life; it told the awesome story of how something came to be or what its destiny held. The figures in the myth could be historic persons, they could be symbolic, or they could be both.

The myth pointed to new realities as they emerged in a new cosmic situation or primordial event. It presented reality as an organic whole, not subject to decomposition. It offered divine persons with whom man could identify and patterns of action that he could emulate. The archetypal figures were both victims and victimizers; they created, destroyed, sustained, and redeemed. Their actions gave man a universal pattern in which to participate, and he participated in such a cosmic drama with fear, hope, awe, wonder, and delight. Believing in and relating to a myth was not understood as an elective choice, for exclusion from the cosmic drama meant emptying human existence of meaning and shrinking it to the speechless isolation of the self. Deprived of the myth, personal history could only lead irremediably to death and history itself could only turn intolerably upon itself. One of the most splendid of myths was the Biblical drama of salvation envisioned by John in the book of Revelation. The Lamb's victory in the Bible's book of Revelation was understood as a reference both to the historical Jesus who was crucified and resurrected, and to the symbolic embodiment of divine sacrifice and redemption. It was understood as the story of how all things were made new: a new heaven and earth, a new city, and a new perspective between Word and world.

Scientific rationalism tended to demythologize the cosmic drama, desacralize the universe, depersonalize truth, and decompose reality. Creation became physical and chemical process, not purpose; truth became whatever could be scientifically verified; and reality came to consist of bits and pieces that might or might not fit together. To speak in a mythical or poetic way was to the rationalist mind not to be taken seriously. At best it was extravagant speech and therefore incredible; at worst it was an admission of superstition.

Since the scientific revolution, rationalism has continued to pervade Western culture and now has become a dominant attitude. Western man is characterized by his faith that he can explain, verify, and accomplish all things with the faculty of human reason. He needs no myths, no archetypes, and no divine intervention; he needs only his own intelligence. Fear that once was inherent in the relationship to divine beings will be abolished as the curtain of the unknown is rolled back. Awe, wonder, and delight that once were the gifts of surprise will now be furnished by rational planning and explanations that demonstrate the amazing capacities of human reason. One need not associate the awesome sound of an earthquake with the sound of God's presence in the Old and New Testaments, nor does one need to think of the accompanying sound of trumpets to herald a new creation. One thinks instead of the structural deformation in the earth's crust or of the volcanic activity beneath the crust. One is awestruck by the possibility of triggering a volcanic earthquake with a hydrogen bomb exploded at the proper depth at the proper time. One finds security against the earthquake not in divine mercy but in man's ability to erect cities immune to the danger of earthquake—and in man's reasoning power to decide when to employ and when not to employ the device of nuclear fission.

For the churchman acclimated to this element in Western culture, Christianity is seemingly devoid of mystery and offers no truth that reason alone could not infer or affirm. It is simply reasonable for him to be a Christian, given the "common-sense" values of peace of mind, positive thinking, and the church's offer to inculcate moral precepts in his children. He assumes there is a perfectly logical chain of arguments supporting many of the church's doctrines, and only tolerance is required where the pastor or theologian fails to make the rationality of the Christian case clear to the modern mind.

As a consequence, the church leader feels himself under severe pressure to show the reasonableness of the Christian faith and teachings. He feels obliged to speak a language that is culturally accredited: the language of logical, discursive speech. Since myth is discredited as unscientific and illogical, he is urged to avoid it, and the church corporately is encouraged to disown it. In his search for a language that is convincing, the church leader appeals to reason and he struggles to clear his terminology of the incongruous and the mythical. Rationality is the criterion for preaching in any congregation of people geared to the dominant motifs of Western culture. At Easter, the resurrection is preached less as a miracle to be adored than as an event to be explained in reasonable, logical terms. Sermons are constructed like essays and the appeal reflects the rationale of salesmanship. Influential books on preaching, such as James A. Pike's *A New Look in Preaching*, urge the preacher to heed the techniques and principles of modern salesmen. Pike speaks of the importance of a market survey before marketing the gospel to the congregation; he speaks of the gospel and sermon as the "product and its packaging," the preacher as the "salesman," and the church as the "store."[3]

For years, theologically competent churchmen have been retreating from the mythical language of Scripture under what they have detected as the subtle but relentless pressure from their congregations to market the gospel for quick, palatable consumption. This reductionist demand means finally that in order for the congregation to buy the product, it must be drastically "modernized."

In their hasty bid for modernity, Protestant churchmen are, in effect, returning to the dictum expounded by Jeremy Bentham and John Stuart Mill more than a century ago and by Thomas Hobbes three centuries ago. Hobbes led a movement toward banishing metaphor from human language. Under the banner of scientific rationalism he labeled the metaphor as unreliable and extravagant. Thus poetic lines like the following were to be acknowledged as absurd:

> 'Tis the spring of souls today:
> Christ hath burst his prison.[4]

They were absurd because spring refers to a season, souls to a metaphysical or religious concept. They were absurd because Christ was put into a tomb, not a prison. As a statement it is not to be taken seriously. In place of metaphorical language, Hobbes offered an emphasis on classification and codification. This was to be a universal language whose meanings were known in exactly the same way by all persons using the same or intertranslatable languages.

Jeremy Bentham further advanced the claim for scientific language as being the only "true" language. John Stuart Mill offered a defense of metaphorical language on the grounds that it was the "expression or uttering forth of feeling." But in offering this defense, Mill damned the metaphor with faint praise, for his critical theory left it shackled before the ascending sway of scientific rationalism. In his theory, poetry could be appreciated in a subordinate role, but the role was stigmatized as the logical opposite of "matter of fact or science." Even Hobbes had left a place for metaphor, but its function was the trivial and unimportant one of "playing with our words." Under the influence of Hobbes, Bentham, and Mill, language tended to divide into two kinds. On the one hand, there was the unassailable scientific statement whose truth was verified by its correspondence with the fact to which it pointed. On the other hand was "emotive utterance" or "pseudostatements" made by poetry, fiction, and religion.

The denigration of metaphor is the linguistic counterpart of the denigration of myth. The churchman today who claims to be speaking the language of the modern layman may mean that he is shunning technically theological jargon; but at the same time he is usually opting for a kind of Hobbesian nonmetaphorical, nonmythic speech. Like Hobbes, he believes he has come close to a universal language. But the Biblical language depends upon metaphors and symbols that cannot be reduced to nonmetaphorical synonyms and upon myth that cannot be restated in propositional, apodictic ways.

Amos Wilder has rightly insisted that the first-century epic of salvation cannot be translated into more contemporary language without loss, regardless of the interpretation necessary to guard against a literalistic understanding of early Christian imagery. When all is said and done to fulfill the inevitable task of modernizing the Biblical language, we still must face the fact that the original imagery of salvation has intrinsic worth: "The symbol and the myth of the New Testament instruct us as to aspects of reality attained in the course of Israel's experience as taken up and corrected and illuminated in the Christ-story. . . . We thus vindicate the intrinsic importance of the early Christian rhetoric in its aspects of imagery. The new myth-making powers of the Christian movement meant more than an overthrow of rival myths and more than a liberation from letter and law. It meant the portrayal of the real nature of things and of the course of existence so far as human speech could encompass such mysteries."[5]

The selection of Scripture passages to be read and expounded at worship services is an instructive barometer of how the cultural climate has registered in the church and how that pressure has affected its language. The book of Revelation, which stands unparalleled in the New Testament canon for its portrayal of the cosmic sweep of the resurrection victory through time and space, has been all but dropped from the denominational lectionaries. The mythic and archetypal language of John dramatizes the universality of Christ's victory in the crucifixion-resurrection event, projecting it onto a broad cosmological screen. The screen is so broad, the universality so complete, the ultimate reality so pronounced, that only the mythic dimension would do justice to the event. But today the modern mind is predisposed to discount such ancient cosmological images and to deny the authority of myth. Therefore the book of Revelation is scarcely acceptable as a source for Scripture passages, much less for texts in preaching. The implications of this eclipse are serious for the church as it has traditionally understood itself and its gospel. Because the book of Revelation provides an access to the full meaning of the resurrection that is not possible otherwise, the Christian gospel arises out of it and is dependent upon it. As Ernst Käsemann, German New Testament scholar, writes: "Early Christian apocalyptic is the mother of Christian theology."[6] For this reason (which will be more fully argued in Chapter 3), the book of Revelation will be the major focus for measuring and evaluating the church's surrender to a rationalist attitude.

Let us examine the evidence supplied by lectionaries of The Methodist Church, United Presbyterian Church, Lutheran Church in America, and Protestant Episcopal Church. Even if the lectionaries are not followed rigidly by parish ministers, the choice of passages represents a certain national consensus, since the committees commissioned to draw up or revise a lectionary include as many, and usually more, representatives from parish churches than from seminary and university faculties. If we take the morning worship service as the common denominator, putting aside vesper services and weekday saints' days as variables too difficult to evaluate accurately, then we find a striking similarity in the picture presented by the four lectionaries. In a year, passages from the book of Revelation appear in the following frequency:

Methodist—once
Lutheran—not at all!
Protestant Episcopal—once
United Presbyterian—twice

In the case of the Lutheran, Episcopal, and Presbyterian lectionaries, the infrequency is even more astonishing because those lectionaries require two readings from the New Testament each Sunday morning, commonly designated "Gospel" and "Epistle." Thus out of a possible 104 readings from the New Testament on Sunday morning, a passage from the book of Revelation is read not at all in the Lutheran church, only once in the Episcopal, and twice in the Presbyterian churches.

The choice of those few passages is also instructive. For its one lectionary passage, The Methodist Church chooses Rev. 19:1; 4:6–8. The verses avoided in this section are verses referring to judgment, to fear, and to the image of the "great whore." The verses chosen are those which form a liturgical song of praise. Similarly, the Episcopal passage is Rev. 4:1–11, a passage limited to two songs of praise, one so liturgical as to be a Scriptural source of the Sanctus. The picture in the fourth chapter alone is one of heavenly worship, with no conflict depicted. But with the absence of conflict goes the absence of any significance in the Lamb's victory. Therefore the resurrection imagery is sundered from the context of the rest of the book, which is one of struggle and ultimate triumph. The same observation could be made about the second passage listed in the Presbyterian lectionary: Rev. 21:1–4. This is a picture of the new heaven, the New Jerusalem, devoid of struggle or conflict. While the picture is rich in imagery, the images do not of their own accord point toward the antithetical symbols with which the Apocalyptist had also been wrestling in his vision, for example, the old heaven and earth, Babylon, and the Satanic beast. (Neither the Old Testament lesson nor the Gospel lesson offers much help in pointing up the struggle from which the victory had been wrested in the portrayal of ch. 21:1–4.)

To the extent, then, that the lectionaries of these four denominations are barometric, we can say that the book of Revelation has all but ceased to be treated as canon in the Sunday-morning worship services. Since the Sunday-morning worship service is still the most climactic "moment" in the life and self-consciousness of the church, this fact serves to point up the disrepute into which the book of Revelation has fallen in the consciousness of modern churchmen. Statistics could also be cited to show the relative obsolescence of the Apocalypse in the teaching process of the churches. In one of the most influential among American Protestant curricula, the *Christian Faith and Life* curriculum, the book of Revelation constitutes approximately .01 percent of all Scriptural references assigned to be used in conjunction with the morning lesson.[7]

The adult curriculum magazine, *Crossroads*, prescribes 104 passages from the Bible for the year 1965–1966, and not a single one is taken from the book of Revelation. The adult curriculum is less significant, because the formal teaching of adults is itself becoming a peripheral part of the church's life.

But this very decline of adult education further accentuates the problem of the church's language. The church is a community of common language, and its continued existence as a church depends upon the ability of its members to communicate in a distinctive idiom. This is a sociological maxim as well as a theological reflection upon the intrinsic value of the gospel's language.[8] The sociologist reminds us that no community can survive if it loses its unique language; at the same time the theologian warns that we cannot share the faith perspective of first-century testimony to Jesus Christ unless we are prepared to hear and speak the new language to which their gospel gave birth. That language depended primarily upon figurative rather than nonfigurative speech, and many of the symbols—such as the cross, the Lamb, the crown, the vine, the New Jerusalem, the bread and wine—are irreducible to nonfigurative speech. They are images through which the gospel was conceived and without which it is bound to be impoverished. They are part of the unique language of the church. The teaching ministry historically has been indispensable to directing and renewing the commerce between the intrinsically important Biblical images and the currency of images that circulate among church members. It is no less dispensable today, given the cultural images and myths of success, money, sex, health, and fame that bombard church members daily through our mass media. Yet, in point of fact, a formal teaching process for adults is fast disappearing from the mainstream of Protestant churches.

The preaching ministry has suffered no such decline, but it is of liturgical necessity a monologue, offering little chance for a genuine dialogue between the language of the gospel and the parlance of culturally conditioned church members. Without being able to communicate in the language of the apostolic faith, the churches can scarcely hope to evoke and nourish apostolic allegiance to Jesus Christ.

Social action has been cited as the locus of creating this allegiance. But social action alone does not interpret the Christian call to discipleship. In fact the basis for the action is rarely understood in a language and idiom unique to the church. Social action is a vital part of the total interpretive process, but it cannot supplant the concentrated exposure to the language of Scriptural witness. Each must vivify and interpret the other.

It is worth noting parenthetically that one of the few voices at the denominational level to draw attention to the once indispensable language of the Apocalypse has come from the social action (urban and industrial ministries) wing, not the "education" wing, of a major denomination. For example, George E. Todd, of the United Presbyterian Board of National Missions, has cited repeatedly the difficulty in developing an urban strategy for action with no images in mind that suggest what the city of the future should be. At the same time he has pointed to the wealth of suggestions for the New Jerusalem in the book of Revelation. The Bible, he argues, begins with a picture of an atomistic society and culminates with a picture of a city of "all races, nations, peoples, and tongues" in the book of Revelation. Furthermore, the treatment by the book of Revelation offers carefully depicted images of what the city should and should not be. Such eschatological images are essential to the vision and work of urban missioners.

Since the church is a human community and therefore must commune in some language, it would be accurate to say that the church tends to assimilate its language to that of other communities. It converses in the language of the business community at the time of financial campaigns, and members often respond in the language of the private club by referring to their financial pledges as "dues." The traditional function of the minister in caring for souls finds expression today in the idiom of psychotherapy. Since any human community loses its sense of identity as it ceases to communicate in a distinctive language, it is not surprising that articles about the church's "identity crisis" proliferate in our secular and religious journals.

The church has drifted into these dangerous shallows in part because it has ceased to attend to the uniqueness of its own language, and also because it has badly misjudged the cultural climate. In their haste to eschew the mythical, church leaders have blinded themselves to the usefulness of myth for the analysis of modern culture. Thirty years ago, Reinhold Niebuhr was urging the church to recognize the relevance to much of our cultural rationalism of the Genesis myth of the Tower of Babel. In that story, man attempted to bridge heaven and earth with his own hands and on his own terms. In recompense for his pride, God confused his speech. Rationalism seeks the same independent ascent to what once was the domain of God. Niebuhr warned that rationalism "dreams of a universal language and of a universal culture. But that is merely rationalism's penchant for Towers of Babel; that is the sign of human reason's failure to gauge its own limitations, of its proud and futile defiance of the finite necessities and contingencies which enter into even the proudest edifice of human spirituality."[9] Niebuhr's quarrel was not so much with rationalism as such but with the church which was failing to heed the myth by wedding its language indiscriminately to that of the culture. Instead of learning to speak a universal language, the church may soon cease to speak at all. It is becoming what Niebuhr called a "culture religion" with nothing distinctive to say.

Another myth that offers something of a transcendent perspective for analyzing a fateful turn in our national life is the Greek myth of Prometheus, who stole the secret of fire from the gods. In punishment he was chained to a rock where he was exposed to birds of prey. The myth can personify the ambition of a nation to possess a secret that can ignite a continent by nuclear fission.[10] Like Prometheus, we can muster a rational argument in defense of our "theft" but may not be reasonable enough to survive the secret. The power and pride that it offers may be too seductive for rational argument to contain. It is important to note that the venture was undertaken by a generation of men, not by a few scientists in the laboratory. The insistence by Congress that half of the national budget be devoted to building a nuclear arsenal—and one tending to be greater each year than Administration leaders have asked for—makes the venture a national one, espoused by a whole people. We are a people who have put our faith in our nuclear secret; we are splendidly Promethean. There are signs already that the second half of the myth is also relevant, that we have become immobilized because of our stubborn pride, and made easy prey for smaller nations. Ours is not the only culture in which the Promethean myth lives, but ours is one that can easily identify with the ambition and perhaps the fate of the legendary figure.

In its haste to eschew the mythical in order to tailor the gospel to the modern mind, the church has not only lost an invaluable diagnostic tool, it has woefully misunderstood our age. For our culture feeds upon a host of popular myths and ones that point to a mystic rather than rational temper of mind. The numerous Eastern as well as Western myths which portray man at the gates of paradise nourish the "American dream," the naïve faith in the Great Society, and the aberrant attempts by individuals to achieve paradisal ecstasy through narcotics, alcohol, and sex. The promise of ecstasy in *Tristan and Isolde* characterizes the American teen-age romance which thrives upon the mystic experience that is doomed to figurative or literal abortion. The secret illusion of a double identity, one heroic and one mundane, gives mythic dimension to James Thurber's classic short story, "The Secret Life of Walter Mitty," and to the comic strip, *Superman*. Like Walter Mitty, and like the bland newspaper reporter, Clark Kent, the American cherishes images of himself as a superhero, unrecognized by the humdrum world of family and work. Finally, the novels of F. Scott Fitzgerald and Theodore Dreiser, and especially Hollywood movies in their own way, have portrayed the archetypal American as the man possessed of a mystical faith in wealth and innocence.

The myth of innocent affluence in this culture owes much of its origin to an Americanization of the apocalyptic myth. Many of the Massachusetts settlers came to embrace the new land as a millennial paradise, the fulfillment of the promise in the book of Revelation that Satan would be bound for a thousand years, ushering in the Kingdom of God on earth. John Cotton and Thomas Goodwin both wrote in commentaries on the book of Revelation (1639) that America was unquestionably the place for the millennium to begin, an event that they regarded as imminent. Samuel Sewall gave fresh credence to the notion in his *Phaenomena Quaedam Apocalyptica . . .* (*De-*

scription of the New Heaven . . . to Those Who Stand Upon the New Earth).[11] Christians who fled the bloodstained establishments of Old World Christendom began to see in America the millennial hope of a new beginning, mercifully cut off from the sinful past. The secularization of the millennial hope encouraged acquisitiveness in the settlers who rolled back the Western frontier. The Great Awakening brought the notion conspicuously to the foreground of the American mind. The Awakening was, as Jonathan Edwards wrote, "the work of a new creation. . . . The New Jerusalem in this respect has begun to come down from heaven, and perhaps never were more of the prelibations of heaven's glory given upon earth." Edwards was convinced that "temporal prosperity will also be promoted by a remarkable blessing from heaven."

Americans have never ceased to seek prosperity as their promised "blessing from heaven," and the myth has survived in contexts which have little to do with Jonathan Edwards or his theology. On a variety of theological and nontheological terms the American came to understand himself as the recipient of a divinely granted renaissance of the human race, standing before the dawn of a new history in a new land full of vast wealth and potentialities. America would never be without her mythic frontier, with gold to be mined, a physical universe to be harnessed, and a paradise to be recognized and enjoyed. As H. R. Niebuhr's classic study of the Kingdom of God in America points out, the millennial hope was "nationalized, being used to support the feeling of national superiority and of manifest destiny. It was confused with the progress of industrialism and capitalism. . . . It was used to justify war and violence. . . . But even these abnormal forms of the hope indicated the power it had over the minds of American Christians."[12]

By the latter part of the nineteenth century the amassing of wealth took on a mystique of both innocence and holiness, for the wealth was the produce of a new creation isolated from the guilt of history and made available to all diligent, positive-thinking citizens of the Kingdom. The millennial paradise offered "acres of diamonds" (the title of an $8,000,000 sermon),[13] to those who had eyes to see and ears to hear. Poverty was for those who were blind and deaf to the paradisal promise, especially the immigrants from the Old World and the slaves who should have returned after the Civil War. There was nothing the millennial Kingdom could not provide for its true citizens, or so the wealthy and the would-be wealthy believed. The myth survived even the Depression of 1929. F. Scott Fitzgerald's famous line in "Babylon Revisited" is a fitting epitaph for the stubbornness of the native American myth: "The snow of twenty-nine wasn't real snow. If you didn't want it to be snow, you just paid some money."[14]

Blind to the myths that tenaciously grip American culture, the churches have repudiated the great mythic images of the Bible. In doing so they are forfeiting the chance to bring to the culture a word of judgment and healing. Rationalistic pronouncements on sex, prejudice, and poverty fall on deaf ears where the hearer is captive to a cultural myth whose mainspring is basically irrational. Yet the churches continue to drone their sterile deliberations in the adopted tongue of the liberal rationalist, whom they have mistaken for the archetype of modernity. They have suffered a failure of nerve and a failure of vision. They have lost the nerve to speak in the native tongue of symbol and myth, and they have failed to see the mythic life stirring behind the cultural masks of rationalism. Ironically enough, they themselves are judged by the myth of Babel for the proud illusion that they can continue to build upon a universal, nonmythic language. As a result of their delusion, they have no word to speak which will either judge or transfigure the mean and tawdry myths that populate our dreams with expectations which reality will never satisfy.

2

THE LOSS OF MOBILITY

One half of humanity battens and grows strong on a doctrine fabricated by human reason; the other half sickens from the lack of a myth commensurate with the situation. ... Christianity slumbers and has neglected to develop its myth further in the course of the centuries.—Carl G. Jung.

FORFEITURE of the Biblical mythology has not only robbed the church of principles of discernment, it has also deprived Christians of the power of action. In his fine discussion of "pre-ethics," John R. Fry has spoken of the "immobilized" Christian,[15] whose plight does not lie in what he should or should not do as a result of his commitment to Jesus Christ, but in how he can find enough psychological mobility to undertake *any* course of action. The established schools of Christian ethics have failed to give sufficient cognizance to the privacy of the mind, which is so disordered and secretive as to be unresponsive to logical prescriptions for action. A man who is governed by a private world where irrational factors hold sway is only further frustrated, and indeed immobilized, by such rational appeals to Christian ethics. He can assent to their soundness or to their daring, but he cannot act upon them because he is immobilized from within. He is immobilized by inadequate or conflicting images of himself, his marriage, his church, his world, and his God. He acts not in accordance with ethical insight, but according to a preexistent image—perhaps his alter ego, perhaps his superego, or perhaps an *imagined* action. If he cannot see himself in his mind's eye in the role that is called for by the prescribed ethic, he will not undertake it. The image must be present before the prescription can elicit a behavioral response. This, in short, is what Fry means by pre-ethics. He argues for the necessity of providing the Christian mind with a "sponsoring fund of images" that will "move with incredible swiftness onto the internal screen of the Privacy as an invitation to action."[16] He calls on the Christian ethicist to give utterly serious attention to the imagination. For "what is needed before . . . the strictly conceptual relation of love to justice, or justice to law, or law to love is set down, is assurance that the Christian public has an overflowing abundance of images that are specifically recallable onto their internal screens. Then the image-making that is inevitably the prelude to responsive action will be appropriately pre-inprincipled, or turned inside out, pre-contextualized."[17]

What Fry means by a plurality of "images" needs careful definition. It is much more than a conglomerate of favored images, insinuated into a conglomerate of unfavored images. Rather, it must be mythoid or productive of myth. If man is immobilized because other images are telling him a story that conflicts with Christian ethics, then the "sponsoring fund of images" which Fry wants to give him must also tell a story—a story more congenial to the action being recommended. This is implied by his illustrations, which depend heavily upon modern fiction. He points out that "the images he [the reader] receives in fiction return to him in surprising ways and at surprising times. They re-*happen* [italics mine] for him across his internal screen."[18] He cites a passage from Nathanael West's *Miss Lonelyhearts.* The scene is a flashback to college days when the protagonist and some friends set out in a drunken spree to slaughter a lamb in parody of the black mass. The attempt to kill the lamb was unsuccessful and the lamb escaped, wounded. Fry's analysis is as instructive as any in his book:

> When the drunken boy in the grass had a definite image of that dying lamb who had *gotten away,* and was mobilized by that image to finish the job, he was not being merciful to animals, he was finishing up the black mass. He was, in short, protecting the human race, himself in particular, from "Christ," by killing the lamb.
> Here we find revealed with startling effect the precedence of image-making over action, *and* the influence of the idea region in sponsoring images, *and,* also, the definite way in which the past comes back, not from the direction of the past, but from the direction of the future! The creating of images, from which the Privacy takes action, actually bestirring himself, lifting his arms, moving his legs, talking, grasping, and so on, is profoundly consequential. Imagination, we see, then, to be more than the mere appearance of mobilizing images, and more than reaction to images coming into the Privacy. Imagination is a creative activity in which the idea materials push forth images of what to do, selecting out from its almost unlimited fund of memory images . . . the appropriate and immediately pertinent image.[19]

It is clear that Fry intends the word "image" to apply to irreducible, archetypal symbols, as well as to metaphors and word pictures whose reference is only private. While he himself is not explicit in differentiating between different kinds of "images," the category of myth and archetype is presupposed.

In the light of Fry's argument it would be difficult to exaggerate the importance of the book of Revelation for mobilizing the Christian man. It offers an abundance of archetypal symbols "from its almost unlimited fund of memory images," reaching back into the entire tradition of the Old Testament. The mythic pattern achieves a startling effect in "the definite way in which the past comes back, not from the direction of the past, but from the direction of the future." Its images are not taken from everyday life such as those we find in the Synoptic parables, but they are not for that reason less relevant for action. Images which a man in his privacy may need more desperately than any others are just those which project a cosmology of time and space. With those images he can enact a universal drama; without them he can be hopelessly immobilized.

To say that a Christian living in the second half of the twentieth century needs such cosmic images of time and space to escape bondage to linear time finds supporting evidence in the novelist's decision for mythic rather than chronological patterns of action, in the cubist development of painting, and in the existentialist protest in philosophy.

The American has been described, convincingly, as a creature for whom space means freedom, and time, bondage.[20] Time has been equated with history, which Americans have always fled. History has been the guilt-laden past of the Old World, from which America promised a millennial break. In America "history is bunk," as Henry Ford is reputed to have said. Americans have never wanted a consciousness of time, and they have never had it. They have had space instead. They have used time to fill the space of an empty continent. Now that the space is nearly filled, we are a nation whose cities know hysteria and whose freedom, historically equated with space, has to be radically reevaluated. To this extent the American is the reverse of his European ancestor, whose space was hemmed in by national boundaries but whose time was the liberating consciousness of myth and ritual that could reenact a cosmic drama of salvation year after year. The time of the family, of the nation, and of the church was deeply meaningful. It was cherished and remembered, celebrated and sanctified. Without time and now without space, the American is a lonely creature; he is without memory or redemptive myth, and he is hemmed in by urban sprawls.

The urgency of this need may also account in part for the soaring popularity of Teilhard de Chardin. While his impact on the modern mind is more commonly attributed to a bold synthesis between science and religion, this entente with Darwinian rationalism also offers a way of dealing with the problem of time. Sensitive minds have not overlooked the offer and its appeal. Robert T. Francoeur wrote an article in 1961[21] entitled "For Teilhard, No Flight from Time," in order to applaud Teilhard's brave attempt to face rather than to escape the inexorable fact of finite time. Francoeur draws attention to the fact that the modern mind considers time "as something we must flee and escape, since it can lead us nowhere. We must either demolish it—petrify it, so to speak—or at least render it completely foreign to our consciousness." He pays tribute to Teilhard for elevating eternity far above "a reward for patiently enduring the unbearable finiteness of time," since eternity for Teilhard is "the pleroma flowing out of time and through it." Teilhard is not John the Evangelist. But the boldness of his cosmic vision of Christ, and the effect which that vision has had on his readers, may indicate some of the "mobilizing" power of John's imagery, once *his* readers can encounter the images afresh.

Another set of images that can liberate the immobilized Christian are those which reveal, as only imagery can reveal, the deceptiveness of the Satanic forces. The similarity in imagery between the beast and the Lamb—between the Whore-Babylon-Rome figure in Rev., ch. 17, and the Bride-church-New Jerusalem in ch. 21—demonstrates the subtlety of Satanic deception. They unveil the false faces of the church in its worship and witness, and of the secular city in its self-aggrandizement. They drive home to the Christian how easy it is for the false to masquerade as the real. Without this awareness the Christian is unprepared for religious or ethical ambiguity. He is likely to be immobilized by the jolting revelation that his once solid world is really fluid with deceptiveness. (He might read an editorial in a religious journal which tells him that to support the Vietnam war effort is to worship the false god of nationalism (and thus to contribute to an "arrogance of power" not unlike the Babylonian and Roman species). On the other hand, he might hear a minister criticize the peace marchers as false prophets who foster an ethic that is absolutist. Even before seeing the dilemma appear in a dramatic issue, he has felt defeated by a religious imperative for a clear decision where no clear perspective exists for making that decision. Once confronted with archetypal images that confirm the ambiguity which inheres in the very nature of a Christian response, he may be free to do what the ethicist and theologian would applaud: to watch constantly for equivocation, yet choose and act with a certain abandon, knowing that we live by grace and forgiveness. In short, we are free to be proved wrong and to fail.

A third set of images that may bring mobility to the Christian is the group we are most embarrassed to display: those of upheaval, destruction, and anguish. To the extent that such images are excluded from the limited stock inherited from Sunday school days about a benign God and a mute, passive Lamb, one has no story or myth that can integrate the terrible with the meek. With the absence of such a myth goes much of the "pre-ethical" equipment for action, and what is left may further immobilize the Christian: an irreconcilable *conflict* of images. If the Christian's sponsoring fund of images is limited to shepherds peacefully keeping their flocks by night and a placid face of Jesus tacked to church school bulletin boards, he is doomed to inner conflict and immobility. For these images are not easily reconciled with the images of race riots, intercontinental ballistic missiles, and psychopathic murders which confront him each day in the newspapers. Nor are they reconcilable with the rage he may feel toward his wife, his employer, or himself. On the other hand, if his fund of images includes the apocalyptic horrors that accompany the cosmic struggle between Satan and the Lamb, he may recognize the call for endurance issued to the Christian who is caught up in this struggle and find in this call an invitation to share the Lamb's victory. In short, he may be able to integrate the full range of his fund of images sufficiently to answer the call and become mobilized for active Christian witness.

Perhaps no one has applied more passionate and disciplined study to this problem in its psychological dimension than Carl G. Jung. As a psychiatrist he was struck by the way Christians were repelled by the Apocalypse and consequently deprived of archetypal images that could mean for themselves and for their culture the difference between sickness and health. He wrote:

> Later generations could afford to ignore the dark side of the Apocalypse, because the specifically Christian achievement was something that was not to be frivolously endangered. But for the modern man the case is quite otherwise. We have experienced things so unheard of and so staggering that the question of whether such things are in any way reconcilable with the idea of a good God has become burningly topical. It is no longer a problem for experts in theological seminaries, but a universal religious nightmare, to the solution of which even a layman in theology like myself can, or perhaps must, make a contribution.[22]

Jung distinguishes between signs and symbols. A sign is that which has a logical equivalent, e.g., a mathematical figure, or an image whose referent can be known apart from the image, as a nation can be known without its flag. A symbol, on the other hand, is an image which has no logical equivalent and whose referent is unknowable apart from the image itself. A symbol is irreducible to logical stipulation. The Lamb image in the Apocalypse is an example, and Jung makes repeated reference to it. On the other hand, the 144,000 can be known apart from the mark of the name on their foreheads (Rev. 14:1), and therefore the mark of the name is only a sign.[23]

From the standpoint of psychology, symbols fall into two categories. The first includes symbols originating in the personal unconscious. They are personal because we can detect their presence and their origin in our individual past histories.

But in addition, Jung insists there is a second category: those originating in the "collective unconscious," in other words, archetypal symbols. These "do not originate in personal acquisitions but in . . . the inherited brain-structure. These are the mythological associations—those motives and images which can spring anew in every clime and age, without historical tradition or migration."[24] Nearly all the symbols in the Apocalypse either are, or have strong affinities with, archetypal symbols, according to Jung's definition. They are archetypal in addition to their particular coloration derived from the history, culture, and the religion of Judaism and early Christianity. The color symbolism of white has universal connotations of purity and sanctity apart from the resurrection of Christ, just as the expression "looking down from heaven" has spatial connotations of deity more universal than the Hebrew-Christian understanding of heaven and angelology.

Jung describes the therapeutic value of symbols in terms of their "effective work" in integrating the personality and thus freeing or mobilizing the person. They accomplish this in two ways. First, they synthesize the opposition between the conscious and the unconscious. When a person represses a reality that is too disagreeable or incompatible to acknowledge consciously, he creates an unhealthy conflict between his consciousness and unconsciousness. He dissociates the disagreeable from the agreeable and thereby invites disharmony between his conscious and unconscious. The conflict between the two may worsen to the point of schizophrenia. Because the symbol can contain conflicting elements, it can work to harmonize the agreeable with the disagreeable. This integration affords the wholeness that is necessary for a free individual. For example, if the conflict-ridden Christian could recognize himself in the symbol of Peter, who was both faithful and unfaithful, believing and unbelieving, he could be a whole person, mobilized for action. A symbol can also have therapeutic value for a community or society. A society can be subject to the same process of repression and dissociation, becoming what Jung calls "a veneer of civilization over . . . a brute." Nazi Germany would typify such a society, while Salem, Massachusetts, during the witch-hunts of 1692, or Chicago during the race riots of 1966, would exemplify such a local community. If Nazi Germany in the 1930's could have recognized itself, as Thomas Mann recognized it, as the personification of Faust (*Doctor Faustus*), its collective psyche might have gained knowledge of where it was heading. Instead, a whole society repressed what was not compatible with the national self-image of Germany.

Secondly, the symbol, especially the archetype, has the more passive function of channeling otherwise dammed-up psychic energy. It can shape and direct our explosive emotions, which otherwise would erupt in chaos or breed sickness from their shapeless repression. The archetypal symbol "is like a deeply graven river-bed in the soul, in which the waters of life, that had spread hitherto with groping and uncertain course over wide but shallow surfaces, suddenly become a mighty river."[25] These riverbeds are latent in the unconscious regardless of whether there has been any conscious experience of the symbol. They are part of the collective unconscious of the human race, which every man inherits. They are organic to the psyche and cannot be disposed of by rational explanation. In fact, serious psychic damage can result from attempts to explain them away and disrupt their normal organic functions. Jung observes that "whenever a projection of these archetypes is destroyed by rational criticism, the disembodied image returns to its origin, the archetype. There it awaits a new opportunity to project itself."[26] The most we can do is "to dream the myth onwards and give it a modern dress." Dreaming the myth onwards in modern dress is highly therapeutic, for it allows for a "perpetual repetition of the law-determined course to take place; since it provides just that character of apprehension or psychic grasp of situations which continually yield a further continuation of life."[27] In fact, Jung goes so far as to claim that the archetypal symbol "represents the practicable formula without which the apprehension of a new state of affairs would be impossible."[28] Thus it is not only futile to rationalize away the archetypal image of the Satanic beast in the book of Revelation; it is unwise, since the apocalyptic myth can give order and meaning to the horror and fear with which we instinctively react when faced with evil in the world.

Like Fry, Jung argues for the priority of the symbol over the purely rational prescription for action. "Reason has never ruled life, and presumably it never will. The questions of life and fate are too often—and perhaps for the largest part—decided by the powers of the unconscious."[29] Therefore, we are urged to grant to symbol and myth the power that belongs to their domain. It is a power that can bring psychic wholeness to a person, a community, or a civilization.

These insights deserve attention. If the church has closed the door to myth because of what it feels to be the pressure of science, it might consider its obligation to reopen the door long enough to explore the claims of one of the branches of science—Jungian psychology. The dilemma that Jung would have the church face is the power of evil. Evil has become visible in the twentieth century and holds us visibly in its grip. We stand mute and helpless before the phenomena of Nazism and Bolshevism, clutching a claim to innocence which has no place in this century. "With glorious naïveté a statesman comes out with the proud declaration that he has no imagination for evil," wrote Jung to a colleague in 1957.[30] The irony in the claim is that only with an imagination for evil can we begin to know what we are dealing with and what to pit against it. Jung explains in the same letter, "One half of humanity battens and grows strong on a doctrine fabricated by human ratiocination; the other half sickens from the lack of a myth commensurate with the situation. The Christian nations have come to a sorry pass; their Christianity slumbers and has neglected to develop its myth further in the course of the centuries."[31]

The "myth commensurate with the situation" is that of the

cosmic drama of salvation in which Christ has done battle with powers and principalities. The myth provided the "imagination for evil" that the early Christians had to possess in order to understand and believe the gospel. Their language was canonized, but their canon now passes under heavy discount where it reflects an imagination for evil. Hence the church is impotent to deal with the demonic realities of the twentieth century, for it will not recognize the myth appropriate to the age:

> Our myth has become mute, and gives no answers. The fault lies not in it as it is set down in the Scriptures, but solely in us, who have not developed it further, who rather have suppressed any such attempts. The original version of the myth offers ample points of departure and possibilities of development. For example, the words are put into Christ's mouth: "Be ye therefore wise as serpents, and harmless as doves." For what purpose do men need the cunning of serpents? And what is the link between this cunning and the innocence of the dove? . . . "Except ye become as little children. . . ." Who gives thought to what children are in reality? . . . I will not discuss the transparent prophecies of the Book of Revelation, because no one believes in them and the whole subject is felt to be an embarrassing one.[32]

Jung's skepticism that the book of Revelation can ever become anything more than an embarrassing subject is warranted by the attitude of the churches, but it is an attitude that must be changed. The stakes are too high for the churches not to rehabilitate the canonical myth from its present state of exile. The book of Revelation may embarrass its readers for a better reason: it presents the scandal of a resurrection faith.

Jung and Fry have both underscored the importance of myth for action as well as for interpretation, for health as well as for faith. The apocalyptic myth provides cosmic images of time and space, an archetypal grasp of the interplay between illusion and reality, and a symbolic pattern that can integrate our imagination for evil within a vision of cosmic struggle and triumph.

3
THE MOBILIZING MYTH

"Behold, I make all things new."—Rev. 21:5.

THE book of Revelation invites the reader to reenact a cosmic drama. It invites him to embrace not only formal worship but life itself as a ritual whose rhythms echo the apocalyptic myth. These are the rhythms of time and space reverberating through the cosmology of history that John has envisioned: we witness, commune, and endure while He comes and comes again. They are the rhythms of illusion passing for reality and then knowledge of the deception bringing reality to light: we waver between uncertainty in deception and doxology in recognition. They are the rhythms of demolition and renewal, the demoniacal cry and the New Song: we bear the ordeal and we share in the triumph of a new creation. An otherwise insignificant life and fragmented world take on mythic shape and cosmic wholeness. The immobilized Christian is offered a vision that integrates his experience of death and life, the diabolical with the redemptive. He is offered complex images with which to identify, images that give radically new dimensions to his gallery of cultural symbols. In this chapter we will examine the images of time, deception, and victory that produce the apocalyptic myth.

I. Images of Time and Space

The victory sounded in the church's ear and projected upon the retina of the church's eye is the resurrection of Jesus Christ. The opening salutation of the book of Revelation invokes the name of Jesus Christ to mean "the faithful witness, the first-born of the dead, and the ruler of kings on earth." As the firstborn of the dead he is the witness to God's victory over the Satanic forces, and therein lies his Kingship. The presiding symbol throughout the book is that of the Lamb who was slain but who is alive and ruling, the crucified One who is the firstborn of the dead. The identification of the historical Jesus, crucified and risen, and the Lamb, slain and alive, is established in the first chapter. Throughout the rest of the book this victory is expanded into a cosmology of time and space. It encloses within its temporal reach God's victory over the primordial forces of chaos (in his act of creation symbolized by the sound of many waters[33]); historical events in the life of Israel (e.g., the song of Moses in ch. 15:3); the life of the seven churches of Asia Minor; and, within the framework of exhortation and promise, the life of the church throughout history (e.g., chs. 21:7; 19:7), and beyond history (ch. 21:1–2). It encloses within its spatial reach the places of Jerusalem, Sodom, Babylon, Egypt, and Rome; the churches of Asia Minor; then by archetypal extension the church anywhere on earth that can be characterized by the citizenship (*civitas*) of the New Jerusalem or the citizenship of Babylon-Rome; and finally, the antithetical realms of the "bottomless pit," the "heavenly Jerusalem." The archetypal images and symbols convey a conflict and victory extended throughout all these temporal and spatial dimensions, but rooted in the resurrection of the crucified Jesus of Nazareth.

Neither the conflict nor the victory is envisioned apart from the participating worshipers who dwell on earth, whether they are worshipers of the Lamb or worshipers of the Satanic beast —and whether they are worshipers in this age or in another.

The worshipers of the Lamb participate in the victory by the "blood of the Lamb and by the word of their testimony" (ch. 12:11). They testify not to their own triumph but to the triumph of the Lamb, the crown of whose victory has been bestowed upon them (ch. 3:11). Their clothing is white raiment, signifying their participation in the resurrection victory. They hear and sing the New Song (ch. 14:3 f.), bear the new name of God and the inscription of the New Jerusalem (ch. 3:12), heed the sound of the trumpet, testify with the "Amen" and the expectant "Come, Lord Jesus!" (ch. 22:20).

John's cosmology of time is one in which events coalesce in accordance with the situation that they reveal in the drama of salvation. Chronology is not the prophet's primary concern. Thus John describes himself to his hearers as "I . . . , your brother, who share with you in Jesus the tribulation and the kingdom and the patient endurance" (ch. 1:9). His link to us is through the commonly shared tribulation, Kingdom, and endurance, a link that can be forged between his time and an infinite number of situations in history. His brotherhood with us is reaffirmed whenever the link is made. The terms on which he establishes his relation with his audience provide a key to his cosmology of time. His mode of projecting time has been subject to one-sided emphasis either upon literal futuristic prediction or upon literal historical commentary limited to the first-century churches. The futuristic interpretation ignores the historical implications, while the strictly historical (first century) eschews the universality of the myth. Both emphases would read into John's perception of reality the primacy which the twentieth-century readers habitually attribute to linear time. John's mode of perceiving time is not ours.

The cosmic drama is not to be charted by our timetables but to be appropriated and enacted daily, monthly, yearly. The millennium, for example, refers to a situation, not primarily to a chronological span of years. "Thousand" is a symbolic number, a multiple of the symbol "ten," which is traditional in

Hebrew thought (cf. "ten horns" of the dragon in ch. 12:3). John's focus is upon the ultimacy of the Lamb's victory, and his concern is with those situations in which the victory is embraced or denied. He is brother to those who suffer for their testimony to Jesus (chs. 1:9; 20:4) and who share the Kingdom through his resurrection (chs. 1:9; 20:4), yet must endure Satan's deception (chs. 1:9; 20:8). His brotherhood was established at the outset and it is reinforced by the account of the millennial situation.

It is with the same sense of brotherhood that he speaks of "the beast that . . . was, and is not, and is to ascend from the bottomless pit and go to perdition" (ch. 17:8). The beast *was*, hence the need for the blood of the Lamb. The beast *is not*, hence the cause for celebration with white garments. The beast *is to ascend* in the illusion of continued reality and power, hence the need to envision the cosmic extension of the crucifixion-resurrection event through all time and space. John is less intent upon locating his audience within a chronological timetable than in describing the nature of the very real battle and victory of the Lamb. He is less interested in predicting *when* the saints shall be clothed in white garments than in affirming that they *are* clothed in the white linen of the Bride: the fine linen is the "righteous deeds of the saints" (ch. 19:8) and in these white garments they will be clothed in the final coming of the Lamb. The corollary to this affirmation is the exhortative beatitude in the following verse: "Blessed are those who are invited to the marriage supper of the Lamb."

In John's cosmology of space it is the archetypal identity rather than the geographical location of a community that is significant. A community can be the City of God or it can be the city of demons, the New Jerusalem or Babylon. The question John forces upon every community in every time is the question of its archetypal species or configuration. Is it the figure of Rome, Sodom and Egypt, or does it have another "spatial" configuration? In the prophet's vision it is possible for a community to combine antithetical figures.[34] Illustrative is Rev. 11:8: "And their dead bodies will lie in the street of the great city which is allegorically called Sodom and Egypt, where their Lord was crucified." This verse makes it clear that Jerusalem can be allegorically Sodom and Egypt because it is the city of Christ's crucifixion, the ultimate in blasphemy and idolatry. At the same time Jerusalem is "allegorically" or archetypally the focal point of God's salvation in traditional Jewish Christian thought, both as the preexistent church[35] and as the eschatological community of the saints (Rev. 3:12; 21:2). Thus one community, Jerusalem, can project archetypal symbolism which is antithetical. The effect of this kind of treatment is to suggest that the battle line extends into the heart of the churches of Asia Minor, which were deceived into believing they were servants of the Lamb when in fact they were servants of the beast. By implication the battle line extends into the heart of our churches today, indeed into the heart of any church and any believer. The choice thrust upon the church is whether that church is going to be the Jerusalem in one figure or the other.

To identify with Jerusalem in one or the other figure is to apprehend reality in a special way that compresses space and time into the archetypal symbol. The Jerusalem that killed the prophets and crucified the Messiah is at once Sodom, Egypt, Babylon, and Rome. Thus John's readers and hearers are asked to make a five-point reference in time and space in order to apprehend the full reality to which the author is alluding. Jerusalem can be Sodom in its blind rejection of the prophets and their message. Sodom was already established in the Hebrew mind as an archetypal symbol of a city's rebellion. Jerusalem can also be Egypt. In Hebrew liturgical and historical consciousness Egypt was inscribed as the archetype of Israel's enemy, the antithesis of God's Kingdom. Jerusalem can also be Babylon. "The great city" is a phrase which John never uses without a specific reference to Babylon, the counterpart of the Holy City, Jerusalem, the City of God. Jerusalem can also be Rome, for all references to "the great city" include a reference to Rome as a part of the Babylon figure.[36] Thus John has reached across geographical and temporal barriers to gather into a multilayered symbol the fullest dimensions of communal self-deception. Such is the wealth of associations that must be apprehended in order to perceive fully an adulterous Jerusalem and an unfaithful church.

To share this vision is to see our time and space freighted with references to historical events and places. These images move in and out of our time in a mythic pattern set forth by John as the universal salvation drama. We are free to be conscious of time, knowing that such consciousness can reveal our role in the drama. History is not sin, as our cultural myths suggest; it is the immense arena of redemption, the vast "moment" for enduring the struggle and celebrating the victory. We are free to be conscious of space, knowing the fluidity of its complexion and its qualitative rather than quantitative importance. Faced with the gradual shrinkage of geographical space, our concern with freedom can turn its focus from the futile question of how much new space a community can occupy to John's question of how "new" or renewed the community is that occupies the space: New Jerusalem and new creation, or old Jerusalem in bondage to Egypt, Babylon, Rome? To live in John's cosmology of time and space is to be mobilized for witness and celebration.

II. Images of Deception

While indicating the extreme either/or of a community's identity, the prophet also presents images of a community that are diabolically similar. In this way he gives full attention to the danger of mistaken identity. He sees the church faced with deception so subtle and complex that the threat is almost more than the church is equipped to cope with or even to recognize. The equipment he offers is a juxtaposition of images whose interplay is parody,[37] and therefore blasphemy. Parody occurs at two levels: Satan employs it in order to blaspheme the Lamb and deceive his followers; John is using it as a literary device to forewarn the "brotherhood" and thus equip them in advance for the arduous discernment that will be required.

The most crucial interplay of images is between those of the New Jerusalem as Bride of the Lamb and the Babylonic community personified in the Great Whore. John describes the New Jerusalem as a "bride adorned for her husband" (ch. 21:2) and then goes on to establish the identity allegorically (vs. 9–10):

> "Come, I will show you the Bride, the wife of the Lamb." And in the Spirit he carried me away to a great, high mountain, and showed me the holy city Jerusalem coming down out of heaven from God.

The Bride's counterpart is the Whore, who personifies the Babylonic community. She is bride to none but prostitute to the "kings of the earth," and she derives her power from the Satanic beast that supports her:

> Then one of the seven angels who had the seven bowls came and said to me, "Come, I will show you the judgment of the great harlot who is seated upon many waters, with whom the kings of the earth have committed fornication, and with the wine of whose fornication the dwellers on earth have become drunk." And he carried me away in the Spirit into a wilderness, and I saw a woman sitting on a scarlet beast which was full of blasphemous names, and it had seven heads and ten horns. The woman was arrayed in purple and scarlet, and bedecked with gold and jewels and pearls, holding in her hand a golden cup full of abominations and the impurities of her fornication; and on her forehead was written a name of mystery: "Babylon the great, mother of harlots and of earth's abominations." And I saw the woman, drunk with the blood of the saints and the blood of the martyrs of Jesus. (Ch. 17:1–6.)

The similarity in imagery suggests that even the "marriage supper of the Lamb," which the Christian community celebrates proleptically in the Eucharist (Sacrament of the Lord's Supper), can be mistaken for its counterpart: the Whore's "wine of fornication" and her "golden chalice full of abominations." The believer, then, is in danger of being seduced by a feast that appears to be truly sacred yet at bottom is profane. The color imagery of purple and scarlet describing the Whore heightens the effect, for it is the color imagery associated with the purple robe of the passion story and with the blood of the crucifixion. Since the Eucharist is the most distinctive mark of the Christian community, just as the marriage supper signifies the true community of the New Jerusalem, by implication nothing else in the identity of the Christian community escapes the threat of deception. At no point can the Lamb's followers cease their vigilance. The threat is not from without but from within the Christian community. Babylon can take shape in the sanctuary of the church; it can form in the church's gathered community postured for worship beneath the trappings of purple and crimson. That very community can prostitute itself to a self-image of splendor and power (of "earthly kings"), and become drunk with the harlot's wine. It can forsake the white linen of the Bride (ch. 19:8) for the jewels and gold and pearls of the Whore (ch. 17:4), only to find one day that it has been beguiled like the Laodicean church: "For you say, I am rich, I have prospered, and I need nothing; not knowing that you are wretched, pitiable, poor, blind, and naked" (ch. 3:17). The Babylonic community is doomed to nakedness and desolation (ch. 17:16).

The temptation to forsake the white linen of the Bride is the temptation to self-worship and self-enthronement: "In her heart she [the Whore] says, 'A queen I sit, I am no widow, mourning I shall never see.'" It is the illusion of independent stature, tempting the community to live not by grace but by its own achievements. It is the lure of impatience with the Bridegroom, the rejection of dependence upon the Lamb (the King of Kings) who alone can enthrone the Bride as a heavenly queen. For John warns of the danger of the community's rejoicing in its liturgical colors, its distinctive markings, as the symbols of cultural prominence and prestige and so becoming merely a culture religion. Once the community has succumbed to that temptation, its goals and fate are mythically foretold.

The imagery of the golden cup and garments of purple and scarlet is intended for more than a Eucharistic reference. While not excluding that reference, the "purple and scarlet" (ch. 18:16) lays the emphasis on Babylon as an archetypal "city" in contrast to the New Jerusalem "city." The whole chapter describes the rhythm of life in a city: buying, selling, trading, weddings, and music. Here it is not simply a woman personifying a city, but the city itself which is clothed in the fine linen of purple and scarlet: "Alas, alas, for the great city that was clothed in fine linen, in purple and scarlet, bedecked with gold" (v. 16). The chapter on Babylon is filled with references to the Bride-Jerusalem figure: the "voice of bridegroom and bride" (v. 23); "in her was found the blood of prophets and of saints" (v. 24); the "kings of the earth" (v. 9), a deliberate contrast to "the kings of the earth" in the New Jerusalem; the gold, silver, precious stones, ivory, bronze, iron, and marble (v. 12), aping the description of the New Jerusalem.

If ch. 18 is so parodic, it raises new questions about the intent of John's parody. With all the violence and holocaust envisioned in the struggle between the Lamb and the Beast, why does John describe the archetypal enemy of Jerusalem with almost a total absence of bellicosity? The city described in ch. 18 is not preparing to make war on the saints. The trumpets (v. 22) are not signaling an attack but are merely entertaining. The images of life in the city are commonplace, except for the city's affluence. The only hint of violence comes in the last verse: "And in her was found the blood of prophets and of saints, and of all who have been slain on earth." The martyrdom mentioned is so extensive, it seems surprising that the judgment pronounced upon Babylon is not more emphatically grounded in this charge ("slaying"). The sin of which Babylon is finally accused is that of "sorcery" (v. 23), and the violence of the "slaying" is treated more as a corollary to that sin.

If we are to take these questions seriously, it is plausible that John is deliberately avoiding the extreme and bizarre imagery that characterizes so much of the Apocalypse in order to draw attention to the allure of these mundane, harmless signs of city life. The "sorcery" (v. 23) need not be witchcraft or a form of black magic; it can be the sorcery of an affluent city, whose affluence becomes seductive. John is pointing to the political, economic, and social order within the archetypal city of Babylon. This is an order which in its corruption bears the guilt of the blood of all the prophets and saints of Christendom. It is an order that has been judged ("fallen, fallen"—v. 2) and a community that burns like the Whore, whose smoke can still be seen (v. 9). The whole chapter adds a note of intense subtlety to the deception characterizing the whore-Babylon-Rome figure, yet makes a resounding affirmation that this archetypal "dwelling place of demons" (v. 2) has been judged and overcome. As the dwelling place of demons, Babylon is a symbol of the old heaven and earth pitted against the new heaven and earth. John is telling his hearers to beware of becoming children of the false mother (ch. 17:5), who buy, sell, marry, sing, only to their own glory (ch. 18:7, 10b, 16), and in so doing not only idolize their community but indirectly perpetrate the slaughter of the prophets and saints.

"The Spirit and the Bride say, 'Come'" (ch. 22:17). And all succeeding generations of believers are enjoined to follow. In their joyful anticipation they look not to the self-glorification of the false queen but to the Bridegroom. The lure of self-enthronement and self-worship can be present in the economic, political, and social orders of the world, or it can be present in the church. John's purpose is not to make a distinction between church and world as we use that distinction today; his purpose is to draw attention to an entire configuration that masquerades as the New Jerusalem Bride. The antithesis may appear in the church, in the world, or in both.

The acts of deception, dividing the hearers from those who do not hear, penetrate the social, commercial, political (ch.

18:23), and religious levels of life. The axis of constant struggle passes figuratively from the millstone (v. 22) to the altar. No person and no church is safe from the peril of seduction. Even churches that have shown exceptional maturity and endurance in discerning false prophets, e.g., the church in Ephesus (ch. 2:2–4), can be seduced into allowing a refined censoriousness to replace the spontaneous love they once had as a communion of believers.

Some church leaders admit that the danger of deception is greater for the Protestant Church in our culture than for the church under some overt form of persecution. But the cutting edge of the Apocalypse drives more deeply than the usual warnings aimed at the acculturated church. The more familiar reaction is to see in the church the appearance of essentially alien forms and behavior and leave off with this observation: e.g., institutional bureaucracy, thinly veiled advertising techniques, modern fund-raising tactics, competition for members consonant with the commercial canons of free enterprise, and the use of statistics. The book of Revelation is less interested in the appearance of things alien to the Christian church than in the forms and behavior which appear to signify the church but in fact do not. The more familiar critique is that there is nothing to differentiate the church from its culture except the shape of the building and its Sunday-morning worship service. But it is precisely in the shape of its building and in the essence of its worship that John would see the greatest danger. There, pride and self-glorification can pass most easily for true worship and thus establish their most formidable stronghold within the church. Today there are few church leaders who fail to detect the appearance of secularism within the church. But not many can detect the presence of self-aggrandizement and falsehood within its specifically religious life of worship and witness. The one is easily corrected, and has been corrected (or overcorrected) by sectarian groups within this country. The other is not so easily corrected, requiring far greater discernment, more arduous and disciplined self-criticism, and an imaginative vision of the nature of Satanic deception. John both gives the reader a detailed picture of cosmic worship and witness, and makes its Satanic substitute point even more precisely to the reality for which it is substituting.

The image of "many waters" is juxtaposed with the same play of irony. Old Testament usage suggests two interpretations of "many waters": first, a chaotic force at enmity with God and yet to be subdued, and secondly, a force overcome and therefore a symbol of victory. The sound can connote cosmic battle or cosmic resolution of that battle. The "many waters," over which the great harlot presides, symbolize a Satanic force, menacing and powerful ("the great harlot who is seated upon many waters"—ch. 17:1). The many waters symbol is invested here not only with the Old Testament suggestion of chaos but with an allegorical reference to thralldom: "The waters that you saw, where the harlot is seated, are peoples and multitudes and nations and tongues" (ch. 17:15). On the other hand, the prophet also hears in the "sound of many waters" a chorus of victory announcing the reign of God and the marriage of the Lamb and the Bride (ch. 19:6–7). The interplay of images invites the reader to distinguish between menace by a Satanic force and the cosmic victory that is wrested from the conflict. He who shares John's vision is forewarned that what he interprets as dragonic threat and bondage may be a "sign" (as the many waters symbol is a sign) not of unending conflict but of ultimate victory. The image can mean seduction by the harlot and despair by the seduced, or it can mean freedom and victory. The question of discernment is one of ultimate significance but fraught with the constant danger of ambivalence.

Again, we are not dealing with mere chronology, as though the reference were to distinctly different time periods with the threat followed in neat sequence by its resolution. For the final resolution of the threat had already appeared in an earlier chapter (ch. 14:2): "And I heard a voice from heaven like the sound of many waters and like the sound of loud thunder." There is little ambiguity in the image of thunder. It is associated throughout the Apocalypse with the Lamb's victory, just as it is associated throughout the Old Testament with God's sovereign rule and awesome presence. Its use in the book of Revelation is particularly reminiscent of the enthronement of the Storm God in the Old Testament, for example, The Psalms and Ezekiel:

> Mightier than the thunders of many waters,
> mightier than the waves of the sea,
> the Lord on high is mighty!
> (Ps. 93:4.)

> And behold, the glory of the God of Israel came from the east; and the sound of his coming was like the sound of many waters; and the earth shone with his glory. (Ezek. 43:2.)

The configuration of the images of thunder and the sound of many waters connote the ultimacy of the Lamb's victory. They appear both before and after the image of the Whore. Hence John is dealing not primarily with sequential narrative but with realities that can be falsely interpreted and therefore need careful scrutiny. The images provide that opportunity and convey the danger of mistaken identity.

III. Imagination for Evil

The prophet entertains liberally what most churchmen prefer to repress: an imagination for evil. The churches' tendency toward repression accounts in large measure for the book's unpopularity. The plagues and woes are brushed aside as the crude ammunition of sectarian groups in their campaigns for proselytizing. On those occasions when ministers do draw attention to the Apocalypse they seize upon the extreme beatific vision at its end, especially at funeral services, when the bereaved need dramatic reassurance. The rare appearances of Revelation passages in the lectionaries for Sunday-morning worship are isolated from their context, and the congregation usually hears the text treated as little more than a brief litany of praise.

The selection of hymns is another case in point. Hymns filled with Revelation imagery of the beatific continue to be popular, while those suggesting wrath or destruction have fallen into disrepute. "For All the Saints Who from Their Labors Rest" has won a reputation as a felicitous choice for funerals, while "Before Jehovah's Awful Throne" has diminished in popularity because it is an incantation of destruction as well as of creation.

It is true that the book of Revelation is filled with doxologies; indeed, it strikes the most resonant note of victory in the entire New Testament canon. But it is *not* true that the woes, plagues, lamentations—the whole grotesquery of evil—is only gimcrackery in John's pattern of imagery. For him the victory is cosmic and substantial precisely because of the grim nature of the struggle. The forces against which the Lamb must contend are so hideous and immense that they defy description, except in the phantasmagoria that he creates. The human community can be victimized by suffering that likewise beggars description in any terms except those of woes, plagues, and lamentations. The imagery is grotesque but not extravagant, given the curse and the degradation to which the human condition is subject. The Lamb's struggle was an either/or of almost unimaginable significance for the inhabited creation and its history. It was a struggle that could not end until even death itself was defeated (Rev. 20:14). It is John's intent to hammer home the either/or that faces his hearers in every generation. Upon the question of their relationship to the Lamb hangs victory or torment, life or death. To attribute less significance to the question is to engage in sham and to be the victim of delusion. A middle ground does not exist for John. One worships the Lamb or he worships Satan—in spite of all the circumlocutions that lay claim to religious neutrality. True worship or idolatry, persevering vision or despair, obedient witness or seduction—these are the choices confronting the hearer. A lukewarm gospel and a halfhearted commitment to the Christian hope are repugnant to him.

The victory is ultimate, but it has been won at a cost. The Lamb unveils no ordeal with which he himself has not been beset as the divine victim sacrificed on our behalf. His followers will reign, but they will also suffer.

Although the trumpet has sounded and its meaning is unequivocal, it remains undetermined who will hear. It is still possible that men will hear only the minstrels and harpers of Babylon (ch. 18:22); men may still chase the illusions of self-glorification (v. 7); they may still surrender any real expectation of a Coming beyond the coming of their redundant death-laden tomorrows. Therefore, the words of prophecy must not be sealed (ch. 22:10) but must be read aloud in the churches (ch. 1:3). If men are truly to hear, to hope, and to long for the coming One (ch. 22:17), they can do so only as their lives and the life of their churches remain oriented to the full vision that John has depicted. It is a vision that ensures their place in an epic triumph and at the same time warns how radical the choice is: to hear it all—the ordeal as well as the triumph—or not to hear anything new; to endure it all or not to endure. Because the victory is cosmic, for all men in all time, the imagery is extreme and its "imagination for evil" is full-blown. But it is controlled by a unified vision and an organic purpose.

The Apocalypse is a "sweet and bitter scroll." It is precisely the images of cosmic victory in time and space which can provide mobility to the believer who otherwise would be incarcerated in himself. The images of upheaval and destruction can provide a mythic context to his own bitter experience in the world. Admitting the diabolical realities about him, he can be mobilized for witness. The Apocalypse is a portrait of deception. The portrait can illumine the universal dimensions of illusion and help identify his role on a cosmic screen.

He who hears the *victory* hears a liberating call to action. He can act in solidarity with the Lamb, marked for the new heaven and earth, no longer bound to the cultural myths about a paradise whose promises have proved empty. In following the Lamb through this universal drama of salvation he will know that he is no longer pinned to a treadmill of repetitive tomorrows, spinning away meaningless time in a spatial prison

—the specter that returns to claim him each time the paradisal promises betray him. From the perspective of the man on the treadmill, a formula for action, however noble and reasonable, is pointless to execute. For the treadmill will soon grind his act into insignificance. But from John's perspective, any man's act can reverberate through the cosmic drama of "following the Lamb" (ch. 14:4), "keeping the commandments of God" (v. 12), and "bearing testimony to Jesus" (ch. 12:17). The reverberative act can sweep through time and space with a significance that the man on the treadmill could never imagine. He can act in concert with the 144,000 who sing the new song before the Lamb's throne (ch. 14:3); his deed can stitch the "white raiment" to identify the true community of the Lamb ("for the fine linen is the righteous deeds of the saints"—ch. 19:8); his seemingly meager action can trumpet the coming of a new creation.

He who lives with the apocalyptic drama of *deception* has a vision of the subtlety and ambiguity of the struggle. He is less likely to be immobilized by the discrepancy between clear norms of Christian behavior and the deceptive realities of life that he encounters. The church's drift into cultural syncretism will call him to vigilance against the wiles of the Babylonic Whore. Others will more easily be seduced and left immobile by the taste of the social status and economic privilege accorded a culture religion. But he will detect the incipient idolatry in a community that is seeking prestige for itself, thereby becoming Babylonic in its self-worship. He will learn to question whether a church lives by grace, content to be the Bride of the royal Lamb, or whether it lives by the pride of its own accomplishments as a queen who has enthroned herself (ch. 18:7). Even in the mundane life of buying and selling, spending and entertaining—in the whole social and economic warp and woof of life—he may be able to discern the Babylonic sorcery (v. 23) which can perpetrate violence and murder. The drive for power, prestige, and racial superiority can be accepted as commonplace—or it can be viewed as the typical mainspring for oppression and violence. The splendor of Beverly Hills, California, can be accepted as an innocent world of affluence and fantasy—or it can be viewed as sorcery that can help precipitate a riot in a neighboring ghetto such as Watts. With epic images of deception giving shape to the patternless world about him, he will be "mobilized" for the epic task of discernment. He will not be unprepared for Babylonic towers growing almost imperceptibly with the mortar of cultural Christianity.

He who hears the *warning* of the Apocalypse and envisions the images of planetary terrors has found what Jung calls a "myth commensurate with our age." He, too, may become a "mobilized Christian." He is free to use an "imagination for evil" in dealing with the realities of life, rather than denying that those realities exist. He is free to view life with a synthesizing vision that only the myth can provide. He will know that he is not in the church to find peace of mind but to "keep the commandments of God and bear testimony to Jesus," and, moreover, he will know that it is precisely this way of life that leads to dragonic warfare (ch. 12:17). That warfare is with a cosmic beast who personifies all that the world once unleashed against Jesus Christ and all that his followers must expect to endure for his sake. It is a battle against Babylon, Rome, Sodom, Egypt—every national and racial embodiment of pride and idolatry. Finally, the images of the plagues that engulf mankind portray the very wrath of God which makes the cross so meaningful. He who breaks the seven seals has Himself endured the torment they depict. He is the Lamb, worthy to be followed and adored in the face of the most dreadful curse, even the curse of death (ch. 20:6). With these images in mind the churches will not shrink from the prospect of struggle; instead, they will shun the peace that is "lukewarm." They will be wary of the undemanding gospel, the false prophets who boast no "imagination for evil," the Babylonic minstrels and harpers that crowd into the darkness every reassuring sound—except the Lamb's trumpets of a new Day.

PART TWO
THE APOCALYPSE AND THE NOVELIST

4

RETURN TO THE MYTHICAL

It [the use of myth] is simply a way of controlling, of ordering, of giving a shape and a significance to the immense panorama of futility and anarchy which is contemporary history. —T. S. Eliot.

WHILE THE CHURCHES have come rather easily to accept the devaluation of mythic and metaphoric speech which they feel a rationalistic culture demands, the literary artists have resisted the pressure for devaluation and challenged the contention that nonmythic language expresses the temper of our time. Indeed, most major novelists and poets in our century have exalted myth as the artist's finest tool for "giving a shape and a significance to the immense panorama of futility and anarchy which is contemporary history."[38]

To be sure, the nineteenth century saw a number of artists who made their peace with the allies of Hobbes, Bentham, and Mill. These artists tended to reconceive poetry and fiction as primarily emotive, cathartic, or, on the other hand, as propagandistic; they were willing to surrender any claims to truth that would conflict with a quite narrowly "scientific" view of language and reality. But the prevailing reaction among artists, especially in this century, has been to reassert the freedom of literary art from scientific language; they have insisted on the autonomy of the literary work of art and thus its exemption from the requirement that it correspond to scientific knowledge and theories. These artists have focused attention on the new sense of reality created by the work of art, not on its exegesis or explanation in logical terms. The work of art *is* something, not simply a fanciful statement *about* something, and on that claim they have stood firm. The "message" enclosed in the work of art cannot be extracted from the form in which it appears without seriously distorting both the artist's intent and achievement.

As one critic has put it, "In poetry we feel no compulsion to refer outside language itself. A poem delivers a version of the world; it *is* the world for the moment."[39] Its whole movement is away from the atomization of reality, and toward its integration. It presents reality in a pattern, a unique matrix of relationships between words and meaning. A new sense of reality emerges from a new way of combining and juxtaposing the words and their meaning. Therefore, one should not ask the poem to mean only something that could be stated more accurately in nonpoetic language. The poem does not obscure reality but presents it as only the poet's imaginative pattern of words can present it. Therefore, the pattern created, however contradictory it seems from a strictly logical or scientific point of view, cannot be destroyed without destroying the sense of reality it claims to present.

Cleanth Brooks and John Crowe Ransom, spokesmen for this viewpoint in literary criticism, have turned to the seventeenth-century metaphysical poets for a legacy of tradition. The poet in this tradition feels himself free to assert boldly his unscientific or miraculous "predications" as an organic whole, fully aware that he is no scientist. His predications are mythic, and myth is "true in the pragmatic sense in which some of the generalizations of science are true: it accomplishes precisely the sort of representation that it means to. It suggests to us that the object (considered in the poem) is perceptually or physically remarkable, and we had better attend to it."[40]

The artistic commitment to symbolism and myth by major novelists in the twentieth century is as radical or even more so than the poet's. For the novelist's decision for myth has meant violating the cardinal principle that plot should be the primary carrier of the action. Shifting the action from plot to a symbolic or mythic pattern has no obvious supporting antecedents, such as those of the seventeenth-century poet. Even the romance, which shimmers between allegory and symbolism in the case of Hawthorne's *The Scarlet Letter,* depends upon plot, the sequence of narrative events, as the principle vehicle for channeling the momentum.

James Joyce and D. H. Lawrence in our century represent the focal points in the development of fiction whose modernity lies in its break from plot. But as turning points they are significantly different. In the brilliantly mythic world of *Ulysses,* the novel encourages a glorious retreat to an inviolable, nearly impenetrable, world of art for art's sake—indeed, craft for craft's sake. In Joyce's novel, art offers what life itself can never provide, since our age has doomed life to be ugly, empty, and philistine. Lawrence, on the other hand, has shown us that Joycean isolation need not be the portrait of all modern artists. The Lawrencean turning point in fiction does not dissipate the stream but redirects it. For Lawrence, art is not vital simply by its contrast to life, but because life itself is vital. For this reason he offered a more hopeful direction to the artist who sees myth as more important than plot, yet who also sees life, not just art, as worth altering; it was a more hopeful course for later novelists who dared again to renew our consciousness of the act of living. By the same token, although both authors contributed to the recovery of myth, it was Lawrence, not Joyce, who helped create a place for the apocalyptic myth in the arsenal of weapons used by contemporary writers for whom life, rather than art, is essentially at stake.

As the critic R. W. B. Lewis has observed, "If Joyce and his contemporaries did turn away from the practical will to live, it was because they turned toward the practical will to create. . . . Art was the answer given back to the first (Joyce's) generation to the universal pressure of death. There was at work something deeper than the ancient formula that art is long and life is fleeting. Life was ugly as well, life was not even lively, not even real."[41] For Lawrence, life was not ugly in either its physical or spiritual form; he hated man's bloodless intellectuality but loved his spontaneity. He bitterly attacked Joyce for intellectual narcissism, which he felt was deadly for the future of the novel. (His reaction to *Ulysses* was to ask laconically whether it lay in a cradle or a death-bed: "Do we bounce with joy thinking of the wonderful novelistic days ahead? Or do we grimly shake our heads and hope the wicked creature will be spared a little longer?"[42]) The strength of Lawrence's attack, justified or not, serves to underscore the radical difference between them. He was passionately insistent that the novel had a future for the celebration of man's life as well as for the memorializing of his art, though admittedly, "it's got to have the courage to tackle new propositions . . . it's got to break a way through, like a hole in the wall."[43]

The Lawrencean revolution brought to the foreground of fiction the *élan vital* of primal, psychic reality that is latent in modern man and resplendent in his universe, if absent from his civilization. In Lawrence's pivotal novel, *Women in Love,* the characters represent the primal drive toward organic wholeness, and the opposing will to possess and to destroy—one thwarted and the other aided by our mechanistic civilization. These psychic forces and their interplay take on mythic proportions. Gerald is portrayed as the false priest, Birkin as the prophet envisioning cosmic communion for men and apocalyptic destruction and renewal for the world. The movement of these psychic forces overshadows the movement of plot with its conventional function of reason (motive) and circumstance (situation).

Ironically, and perhaps significantly, both turning points for fiction occurred in the decade of World War I (1914–1924). The antirationalism in both novelists appeared at a time when the illusion of history's rationality was wearing painfully thin. Both Joyce's *Ulysses* and Lawrence's *Women in Love* (begun in 1913 and published in 1920) represent a complete breach with the Aristotelian doctrine that plot be handled as the primary vehicle for the action, a doctrine first articulated for dramatic literature in the *Poetics* and ultimately canonized for fiction by Henry James. The effect of the shift from plot to myth was to suggest that because history no longer has a rational basis, therefore a rationally ordered plot must be abandoned. The fact that plot is no longer structured chronologically but violates our conventional concepts of time—and with a vengeance—reflects the novelist's view that linear time (*chronos*) is less meaningful than its imaginative compression into the existential moment, or than its expansion into a mythic pattern of time (*aiōn*).

Lawrence's "hole in the wall" opened not only a general mythic vision but a specifically apocalyptic imagination, an imagination nurtured by the book of Revelation. (His original title for *Women in Love* was *Dies Irae*, meaning "Days of Wrath.") His last book was a personal commentary on the book of Revelation, entitled *Apocalypse*. It is not surprising that the strong legacy of Lawrence in modern fiction has inspired an apocalyptic imagination. Post World War II writing, like Lawrence's post World War I novels, has found the apocalyptic myth beyond the broken wall—ambiguous, immense, and commensurate with the age.

Use of the apocalyptic myth by a novelist or poet does not imply a theology, much less the intent to convert or to edify. Behind the art form may be a personal commitment to provide a prophetic mirror to the time in which we live, but that prophecy is not necessarily Christian or even religious in any formal sense. On the other hand, to say that he is an artist without theological commitment or proselyting aims is not to say that his work of art tells us nothing of Christian truth. On the contrary, the novelists who revive the apocalyptic myth provide the reader with insights into the canonical book of Revelation which may have more depth than some of the anemic and evasive commentaries offered by the churches, whose tendency is to rationalize an embarrassing book. By the same token, the novelists may also provide the reader with insights that have little to do with the meaning of the canonical book. But in either case, the vitality that the symbols and images of the Biblical source exert through the novel is remarkable. The engaging "relevance" with which they command the attention of a reading public can be deeply instructive to a Western cultural Christendom which has all but discounted the alpha and omega of apocalyptic language—its images, symbols, motifs, and mythic structure. The apocalyptic myth strikes a sensitive note for a reason the churches have not yet understood: myth has never lain dormant in our culture, it has only been dressed in rationalistic clothing. The churches' own increasingly rationalistic pose tends to blind them still further to the vivacity of myth in our culture.

To give a full picture of the ways in which the apocalyptic imagination has developed in modern fiction is beyond the scope of this book. The fact that it forms a discernible tradition, which we may speak of today as a literary convention, is the salient point. D. H. Lawrence did not initiate the tradition, nor is he necessarily the primary influence in the writings of twentieth-century novelists dependent upon it. He simply gave the tradition a crucial impetus. In America it is Nathanael West who should be called the father of postwar (World War II) "apocalyptic" fiction. He in turn is indebted more to Dostoevsky (*The Possessed*) and Melville (*The Confidence Man*) than to Lawrence. In *Doctor Faustus,* Thomas Mann works out a sustained analogy to the book of Revelation that is unique in modern fiction for its technical brilliance and thematic scope. His claim on the literary mind of our day is also substantial.

Postwar American writers who have continued to mine the

same vein include Ralph Ellison, John Barth, and Thomas Pynchon—all among the most promising, and already critically acclaimed, contemporary writers in America. R. W. B. Lewis has carefully traced this apocalyptic vein in American literature and mapped its recurring contours in a way that is unsurpassed for originality and clarity. In an essay entitled "Days of Wrath and Laughter"[44] he has shown that the major characteristics in this tradition are an Antichrist or Satan figure; a semihero or victim; a narrative progression through certain phases similar to the phases in the book of Revelation (e.g., the state of final apostasy, the loosening of Satan, and then the final cosmic catastrophe); and a tone that is at once savage and comic. The fictive techniques are parody and unbounded blasphemy, perpetrated both by the Antichrist figure and by the author himself. The Antichrist, like the Biblical figure in the Apocalypse, appears in a variety of forms. In the book of Revelation he appears as the Serpent, the Beast, and as Satan. He manifests his power in the Whore of Babylon, in those who commit fornication with the Whore, in all the nations which drink from her "cup of abominations," and in all those who bear the mark of the Beast. In the novels that follow the decisive American text for this tradition, *The Confidence Man*, the Antichrist also possesses the skill of metamorphosis, is the master of deceit and fraud. Lewis suggests there is a root vein of the prophetic which runs through these novels. Beneath all the violence, cruelty, hate, and doom, beneath the laughter born of sheer nausea, is a prophetic aim: "These apocalyptic visions indeed are offered as weapons for averting the catastrophe."[45] All these authors know intuitively what Mark Twain knew: that our human race has only one really effective weapon—laughter (a statement by Satan in Mark Twain's *The Mysterious Stranger*). As Lewis rightly insists, "Satan's metaphor, as apt as it is unexpected, helps to identify the imaginative aim of a series of novels which, over the past two and a half decades, have explored a thickening American chaos, an America hovering ever more perilously on the day of doom.

For while attempting to do full justice to the conditions perceived, these novels have a further apocalyptic purpose—to reveal the essential fraudulence within the horror, to uncover the ridiculous within the catastrophic; in the hope, at least, of letting in a little light."[46]

Not all major twentieth-century writers have turned to the apocalyptic myth, but many of them have returned to myth as the means, and perhaps the only means left, of representing the careening course of modern history. Of these writers a highly significant group have turned to the apocalyptic myth in the book of Revelation for weapons with which to reach, and perhaps to help save, modern man.

5

APOCALYPSE OF SOUL AND NATION:
Miss Lonelyhearts and The Possessed

> *"Not a single nation has ever been founded on principles of science or reason. . . . Nations are built up and moved by another force . . . 'the river of living water,' the drying up of which is threatened in the Apocalypse."*
>
> —Shatov, in *The Possessed.*

IT IS APPROPRIATE to couple the novels by Dostoevsky and Nathanael West. Dostoevsky's legacy is apparent in West, although West's focus in *Miss Lonelyhearts* narrows, like that of so many writers in this century, to the shrunkenness of the human soul. These novels are classic texts for what in contemporary fiction is a typical progression of scope: from the self to the nation and society at large, to history and its meaning.

For both of these authors, the rational basis of history has been undermined. In a sense Dostoevsky was ahead of his time in portraying in the late nineteenth century what nearly all novelists in the twentieth century would have to portray after World War I. But Russia, too, was ahead of her time. The rationalistic liberals of the 1840's spawned a generation of irrational revolutionaries who plunged Russia into an atmosphere of nihilism and holocaust in the 1870's. Russia's plunge prefigured the fate of Western Europe, and Western critics and writers have accepted Dostoevsky as a prophet. This acceptance recognizes in his thrust toward the psychic and mythic a conviction that rational history has quite literally gone to hell. West accepts him on these terms so much so that he does not even bother with a historical dimension to his novel. The absence of the historical element merely accentuates the isolation of the soul, seemingly unaware of time and indifferent to place. What he is concerned with, however, is myth. West, like Dostoevsky, is taken with the apocalyptic myth and turns to it for his weapons. He uses the dark side of the Apocalypse to help create the tour de force of his brief, poignant novel.

Miss Lonelyhearts, by Nathanaël West

West gives us a montage of scenes whose sequence is mostly gratuitous for developing a narrative plot. "Miss Lonelyhearts" is the journalistic pseudonym for a man whose real name is never given. We know only that he is a New England puritan, the son of a Baptist minister. He is hired to write a newspaper column for the lovelorn, doling out pious advice in response to their letters. The column is both an asset for boosting the circulation of the paper and a staff joke, perpetrated by the feature editor, Willie Shrike. As the letters pour in, Miss Lonelyhearts comes to the agonizing awareness that they are genuine cries for help from the pits of human degradation and despair. The stock answer for these cries had been Christ, but Christ was Shrike's particular joke, now turned sour for the columnist. Throughout the novel he remains trapped as the victim of Shrike's blasphemous joke. Shrike plays with his victim as the bird of prey that is his namesake plays with insects, impaling them on thorns. Blasphemy is the particular thorn on which he has impaled Miss Lonelyhearts:

> "Ah, my young friend!" Shrike shouted. "How do I find you? Brooding again, I take it."

> "For Christ's sake, shut up."
>
> Shrike ignored the interruption. "You're morbid, my friend, morbid. Forget the crucifixion, remember the renaissance. . . ." He raised his glass, and the whole Borgia family was in his gesture. "I give you the renaissance. What a period! What pageantry! Drunken popes . . . Beautiful courtesans . . . Illegitimate children. . . . But that reminds me, I'm expecting one of my admirers—a cow-eyed girl of great intelligence." He illustrated the word *intelligence* by carving two enormous breasts in the air with his hands. "She works in a book store, but wait until you see her behind."
>
> Miss Lonelyhearts made the mistake of showing his annoyance.
>
> "Oh, so you don't care for women, eh? J.C. is your only sweetheart, eh? Jesus Christ, the King of Kings, the Miss Lonelyhearts of Miss Lonelyhearts."[47]

The scenes which follow depict Miss Lonelyhearts' struggle to extricate himself. He goes through an odyssey of drink, perverse sex, and an escape to a farm with a girl who loves him. None of the attempts to escape is successful and he is rendered ludicrous by all of them. On the side of love, both for humanity and for Betty (the girl who loves him), he touches a range of redemptive possibilities. But none of them materialize, and his adventures only impale him further on perversion, suffering, and violence. Near the end of his odyssey, he is approached at a bar by Doyle, a homosexual cripple, whom the novelist endows with the subhuman pathos of Dostoevsky's cripples. When Miss Lonelyhearts pays a visit to Doyle's home, and his buxom wife tries forcibly to seduce Lonelyhearts, the effect is both to ridicule Lonelyhearts (who by this time is trying desperately to imitate Christ) and to bring on one of her homosexual husband's fits of madness. In the end, Miss Lonelyhearts experiences a religious conversion during a fever, and believes that God has finally commissioned him to succor the suffering humanity about him. The doorbell rings and he finds the cripple trying to make his way up the stairs, a signal for his real mission to begin:

> God had sent him so that Miss Lonelyhearts could perform a miracle and be certain of his conversion. It was a sign. He would embrace the cripple and the cripple would be made whole again, even as he, a spiritual cripple, had been made whole.
>
> He rushed down the stairs to meet Doyle with his arms spread for the miracle.
>
> Doyle was carrying something wrapped in a newspaper. When he saw Miss Lonelyhearts, he put his hand inside the package and stopped. He shouted some kind of a warning, but Miss Lonelyhearts continued his charge. He did not understand the cripple's shout and heard it as a cry for help from Desperate, Harold S., Catholic-mother, Broken-hearted, Broad-shoulders, Sick-of-it-all, Disillusioned-with-tubercular-husband. He was running to succor them with love.
>
> The cripple turned to escape, but he was too slow and Miss Lonelyhearts caught him.
>
> While they were struggling, Betty came in through the street door. She called to them to stop and started up the stairs. The cripple saw her cutting off his escape and tried to get rid of the package. He pulled his hand out. The gun inside the package exploded and Miss Lonelyhearts fell, dragging the cripple with him. They both rolled part of the way down the stairs.[48]

The polar forces in the author's apocalyptic imagination are the figures of an antichrist, Shrike, and a victim bungling his way toward an imitation of Christ. They are played off in a *dance macabre* that is at once grim and ludicrous. Lonelyhearts' reach for a Savior image lifts him only to the stature of a clown, and he is destroyed by a ridiculous accident. His psychic and physical destruction personifies the catastrophe reserved for the human soul in a world bonded to Satanic power. Like the dragon, the beast, and the image of the beast in the Apocalypse, Shrike commands the weapons of blasphemy, and his tactic is deception.

The author calls upon the dark side of apocalyptic myth to expose the sheer bestiality in some of our most cherished cultural myths. The myths suggesting that psychic and spiritual wholeness can be found through sex or even religious ecstasy are betrayed for what they are—snares of deception set by Shrike, the Satanic beast of prey.

The novel is drenched with images that appear in the canonical book of Revelation. The chapter entitled "Miss Lonelyhearts and the Lamb" is particularly poignant with this imagery as it prefigures the destruction of Lonelyhearts. After reading a chapter from Dostoevsky's *The Brothers Karamazov* Lonelyhearts suddenly decides to make a "millennial" success of his column:

> His column would be syndicated and the whole world would learn to love. The Kingdom of Heaven would arrive. He would sit on the right hand of the Lamb.
>
> But seriously, he realized, even if Shrike had not made a sane view of this Christ business impossible, there would be little use in his fooling himself. His vocation was of a different sort. As a boy in his father's church, he had discovered that something stirred in him when he shouted the name of Christ, something secret and enormously powerful. He had played with this thing, but had never allowed it to come alive.
>
> He knew now what this thing was—hysteria, a snake whose scales are tiny mirrors in which the dead world takes on a semblance of life. And how dead the world is . . . a world of doorknobs. He wondered if hysteria were really too steep a price to pay for bringing it to life.
>
> For him, Christ was the most natural of excitements. Fixing his eyes on the image that hung on the wall, he began to chant: "Christ, Christ, Jesus Christ. Christ, Christ, Jesus Christ." But the moment the snake started to uncoil in his brain, he became frightened and closed his eyes. . . . But no matter how hard he struggled, his prayer was one Shrike had taught him and his voice was that of a conductor calling stations.
>
> "Oh, Lord, we are not of those who wash in wine, water, urine, vinegar, fire, oil, bay rum, milk, brandy, or boric acid. Oh, Lord, we are of those who wash solely in the Blood of the Lamb."[49]

The psychic image of the snake uncoiling to rise at the chant of Christ conjures up the mythic conflict in the book of Revelation between the Lamb and his worshipers on the one hand, and on the other hand, the dragonic power derived from the serpent and delegated to the beast and the image of the beast. The chant itself is a Satanic parody of the liturgical doxologies sung by those who worship the Lamb.

Then follows a flashback to an episode when he was at college, the scene following an abortive attempt to slaughter a real lamb in consummation of the Lonelyhearts' chant. He participates in the mocking episode along with some of his college friends during a drunken spree:

> Steve was sent to the cutlery stand for a butcher knife, while the other two remained to bargain for a lamb. After a long, Armenian-like argument, during which Jud exhibited his farm training, the youngest was selected, a little, stiff-legged thing, all head.
>
> They paraded the lamb through the market. Miss Lonelyhearts went first, carrying the knife, the others followed, Steve with the jug and Jud with the animal. As they marched, they sang an obscene version of "Mary Had a Little Lamb." . . .
>
> Miss Lonelyhearts was elected priest, with Steve and Jud as his attendants. While they held the lamb, Miss Lonelyhearts crouched over it and began to chant.
>
> "Christ, Christ, Jesus Christ. Christ, Christ, Jesus Christ."[50]

Instead of killing the lamb at first, they only wound its head with a misdirected blow. Later the head is crushed with a rock. While the scene is vaguely parodic of the Old Testament imagery of sacrifice, the emphasis is on Christ as the Lamb. The reference to the size of the head and to wounding the head suggests the imagery of the parodic Beast whose head was mortally wounded (Rev. 13:3) as well as the larger motif of parodying the crucifixion of Christ implied in this reference to the beast. The analogy should not be overdrawn, but the parallel motif of mocking the Lamb in parody of the crucifixion is clearly operative.

Shrike's prayers and poems are filled with allusions to the

Lamb and to the "Blood of the Lamb." In one of his last conversations with Miss Lonelyhearts he alludes to the lifelong struggle between the Christ-Miss Lonelyhearts figure and the devil. That life is a gospel which unrolls like a bittersweet scroll. The occasion of the conversation is a letter from the cripple accusing Miss Lonelyhearts of raping his wife and threatening to blow the columnist's brains out in revenge. Shrike comments:

> "How this shakes one's faith! But I can't believe it. I won't believe it. The master can do no wrong. My faith is unshaken. This is only one more attempt against him by the devil. He has spent his life struggling with the arch fiend for our sakes, and he shall triumph. I mean Miss Lonelyhearts, not the devil.
>
> "The gospel according to Shrike. Let me tell you about his life. It unrolls before me like a scroll."[51]

Another fragment in the montage of scenes centers on the imagery of a trumpet and a cosmic cross. Physically sick, Miss Lonelyhearts imagines himself in the window of a pawn shop. He envisions the necessity for apocalyptic destruction:

> Every order has within it the germ of destruction. All order is doomed. . . .
>
> A trumpet, marked to sell for $2.49, gave the call to battle and Miss Lonelyhearts plunged into the fray. First he formed a phallus of old watches and rubber boots, then a heart of umbrellas and trout flies, then a diamond of musical instruments and derby hats, after these a circle, triangle, square, swastika. But nothing proved definitive and he began to make a gigantic cross. When the cross became too large for the pawnshop, he moved it to the shore of the ocean. There every wave added to his stock faster than he could lengthen his arms.[52]

A trumpet sets off his vision of a cosmic cross extending over the sea in a way that recalls the trumpet symbol in the book of Revelation. There the trumpets signal an apocalyptic assault by the forces of the Lamb, effectually extending the victory of the cross into space and time.

The Possessed, by Fyodor Dostoevsky

The train of action in Dostoevsky's *The Possessed* is a revolutionary plot whose goal and method are nihilistic destruction. Pyotr, leader of a terrorist quintet, envisions Nikolay Stavrogin as the messiah to ride the crest of the revolution and inaugurate a new age for Russia. Pyotr idolizes him for the perverse and bloodless detachment with which he regards his world. But Stavrogin hates himself for his perversity and recognizes with increasing remorse that he is an exile from the human community. He is far too aware of his damnation to be seduced by Pyotr's offer of messiahship. In the end, he exclaims to a monastic priest, Tihon, that he loves him for reading a passage from the book of Revelation that rebukes the Laodicean church for being neither hot nor cold. Stavrogin *is* "hot and cold" in one sense, but in another sense he answers the description of the Laodiceans: "wretched, and miserable, and poor, and blind, and naked" (Rev. 3:17). What the priest urges Stavrogin to recognize as repentance, Shatov, another member of the quintet, had also cherished throughout as the greatest hope for Stavrogin. Shatov, from the time of his former serfdom on the Stavrogin estate, had worshiped Stavrogin and sought for him the touch of God and the human community—the polar opposite of Pyotr's hope for him. Shatov and Pyotr break apart within the quintet, Shatov disenchanted with its nihilism. Pyotr finally manipulates Shatov's murder by the group as a precaution against betrayal and as a means of cementing the others in a kind of blood guilt.

On this train of action is freighted social intrigue (scandal), political intrigue (hysteria), and theological intrigue (demonic possession), and we pass through them in that succession. Stavrogin marries a cripple to scandalize his family and insult the social world that had claimed him. The political intrigue gathers momentum with the internal threat of Shatov and Pyotr's determination to destroy him. The theological intrigue arises out of the contrast between Shatov, who passionately believes in the God-bearing people of Russia and their divine destiny, and Kirillov, another member of the quintet, who believes with equal passion that God is a hoax that he can expose by his own suicide. The theological momentum gathers with the deepening of Stavrogin's remorse, which hovers between Christian repentance and despair—until he finally hangs himself.

Stavrogin's actions at all three levels contrast with the response of his former tutor, Stepan Verhovensky. Stepan raised Stavrogin and fathered Pyotr; he represents the whole Russian generation of liberals who spawned a generation of nihilists. Stepan is a foil for Stavrogin, but he is more than that. For the book is the story of a struggle between the two generations —or rather, it is the story of Russia struggling to survive them: the liberal humanism of the 1840's and the dragon's teeth of nihilist mania that they had sown by the 1860's.

The structure of the novel reflects the polarity. In the first part, all the characters are defined by their relation to Stepan; in the second part, all are measured against Stavrogin. Both Stepan and Stavrogin, in turn, are defined by a passage from the book of Revelation, and both share a quasi-apocalyptic vision of a new creation. Both touch in the end as they had when they had once been tutor and pupil: "Stepan Trofimovitch succeeded in reaching the deepest chords in his pupil's heart, and had aroused in him a first vague sensation of that eternal, sacred yearning which some elect souls can never give up for cheap gratification when once they have tasted and known it."[53]

Between them we see Russia, lurching from scandal to hysteria to demonic possession. We move from chaos in the psyche, to chaos in the family, to political chaos, and finally to religious chaos. Chaos at every level has its national dimension. Even religious chaos means national chaos, given Russia's vocation in the novel as the God-bearing people. ("Only one nation is 'god-bearing,' that's the Russian people," Shatov tells us.)

Dostoevsky treats all the characters except Stepan with fierce parody. He treats Stepan with tender irony, for only Stepan had the possibility of "dispossession." But in Stavrogin he incarnates a theme for the nation: that only the great sinner can be the great redeemer. He works out a sociopolitical analogy to this theme in the history of Russia, suggesting that only the nation that has gone through the horrors of the truly demonic can become the God-bearing people. These horrors take on symbolic form in the holocaust of fire precipitated by the quintet as an act of arson and murder; they take on the mythical dimension in which the God-bearing (Russian) and God-witnessing (Biblical) people must endure an apocalyptic rhythm of suffering and rebirth.

To say that *The Possessed* is apocalyptic is to point to more than its volcanic tone. The novel *is* volcanic at the psychic, social, political, and theological levels, and the eruptions are mysterious and enigmatic. (Even Tihon, the priest to whom Stavrogin makes his confession, suffers from what the text describes as "obscure nervous spasms.") But, like *Miss Lonelyhearts,* it is apocalyptic in the very specific sense that it bears reference to the canonical book of Revelation. Immediately behind the stage of its action is the backdrop of the apocalyptic myth.

All the main characters except Kirillov refer explicitly to the book of Revelation, and he, by implication, is the most dramatic representation of the man possessed by Satan, bearing the mark of the beast. He is the supreme blasphemous parody of the Lamb: the God-man mocked by the man-God. In Stavrogin's conversation with Kirillov about his idea of suicide, he cites, "without the slightest irony," the book of Revelation to point out: "In the Apocalypse the angel swears that there will be no more time."[54]

Shatov understands the Apocalypse in national terms. He is obsessed with the idea of an eschatological force, personified in the Russian people, "an insatiable desire to go on to the end," as he calls it. "It's the spirit of life," he says, " 'the river of living water,' the drying up of which is threatened in the Apocalypse." He tries to explain his obsession with this thought:

> "Only one nation is 'god-bearing,' that's the Russian people, and . . . and . . . and can you think me such a fool, Stavrogin," he yelled frantically all at once, "that I can't distinguish whether my words at this moment are the rotten old commonplaces that have been ground out in all the Slavophil mills in Moscow, or a perfectly new saying, the last word, the sole word of renewal and resurrection."[55]

A reference to the beasts of the Apocalypse fittingly climaxes the heated exchange between Pyotr and Fedka, the criminal at large.

The most direct, and in some ways the most important, reference is the one that strikes a deep, reverberative chord in the two main characters of the novel, Stepan and Stavrogin. In each case, it is the identical passage from the third chapter of Revelation. Stepan on his deathbed says to Sofya:

> "Read me something more, just the first thing you come across."
>
> Sofya Matveyevna opened the Testament and began reading.
>
> "Wherever it opens, wherever it happens to open," he repeated.
>
> " 'And unto the angel of the church of the Laodiceans.' "
>
> "What's that? What is it? Where is that from?"
>
> "It's from the Revelation."
>
> *"Oh, je m'en souviens, oui, l'Apocalypse. Lisez, Lisez,* I am trying our future fortunes by the book. I want to know what has turned up. Read on from there. . . ."
>
> " 'And unto the angel of the church of the Laodiceans write: These things saith the Amen, the faithful and true witness, the beginning of the creation of God;
>
> " 'I know thy works, that thou art neither cold nor hot; I would thou wert cold or hot.
>
> " 'So then because thou art lukewarm, and neither cold nor hot, I will spue thee out of my mouth.
>
> " 'Because thou sayest, I am rich and increased with goods, and have need of nothing: and thou knowest

not that thou art wretched, and miserable, and poor, and blind, and naked.' "

"That too . . . and that's in your book too!" he exclaimed, with flashing eyes and raising his head from the pillow. "I never knew that grand passage! You hear, better be cold, better be cold than lukewarm, than *only* lukewarm."[56]

At Tihon's, Stavrogin asks Tihon,

"Have you read the Apocalypse?"

"I have." . . .

He quickly dropped his eyes, leaned his wrists on his knees, and impatiently prepared to listen. Tihon began reciting, recalling word after word:

" 'And unto the Angel of the Church of the Laodiceans write: These things saith the Amen, the faithful and true witness, the beginning of the creation of God; I know thy works, that thou art neither cold nor hot; I would thou wert cold or hot. So then because thou art lukewarm, and neither cold nor hot, I will spue thee out of my mouth. Because thou sayest, I am rich and increased with goods and have need of nothing: and thou knowest not that thou art wretched, and miserable, and poor, and blind, and naked . . .' "

"Enough!" Stavrogin cut him short. "Do you know, I love you very much."[57]

Here upon the same passage from the book of Revelation is the theological issue between Stepan and Stavrogin. The sin of the church of Laodicea, like that of the liberals of the forties, is self-complacency. It is no manifest evil, but a more perilous evil. The Laodiceans were unaware that they were wholly out of communion with Christ and felt no need of repentance. They were serenely unconscious of what they had done and left undone. To Stepan it is only a grand passage from a book by which he is going to "try out our future fortunes." To Stavrogin it is a passage so profound that it evokes from him what nothing but the vision could evoke: the confession of love.

Unlike *Miss Lonelyhearts,* this novel envisions more than the dark side of the Apocalypse. Dostoevsky's apocalyptic imagination is two-sided. At the Dresden gallery, Stavrogin has a dream inspired by a painting which he called *The Golden Age*. While the literal references are to Greek mythology, the analogy to the new heaven and earth in the last two chapters of the Apocalypse is transparent:

> "I cannot quite tell, however, what I dreamed of. As in the picture, I saw a corner of the Greek archipelago the way it was some three thousand years ago: caressing azure waves, rocks and islands, a shore in blossom, afar a magic panorama, a beckoning sunset—words fail one. European mankind remembers this place as its cradle, and the thought filled my soul with the love that is bred of kinship. Here was mankind's earthly paradise, gods descended from heaven and united with mortals, here occurred the first scenes of mythology. . . .
>
> "Oh, how happy I was that my heart was shaken and that at last I loved! The sun poured its rays upon these isles and this sea, rejoicing in its fair children. Oh, marvellous dream, lofty illusion! The most improbable of all visions, to which mankind throughout its existence has given its best energies, for which it has sacrificed everything, for which it has pined and been tormented, for which its prophets were crucified and killed, without which nations will not desire to live, and without which they cannot even die! All these sensations I lived through, as it were, in this dream; I repeat, I do not know exactly what I dreamed about, my dream was only of sensation, but the cliffs, and the sea, and the slanting rays of the setting sun, all that I still seemed to see when I woke up and opened my eyes, for the first time in my life literally wet with tears. I remember these tears, I remember that I was glad of them, that I was not ashamed of them. A feeling of happiness, hitherto unknown to me, pierced my heart till it ached."[58]

The movement from the personal to the sociopolitical to the theological dimensions parallels the movement of the apocalyptic vision in the book of Revelation. The link between John and the seven churches of Asia Minor is the brotherhood of tribulation (Rev. 1:9). His tribulation is the personal trial of exile on the island of Patmos; theirs arises out of the sociopolitical events that have enmeshed them. But their tribulation provides further linkage to the mythic trials of the saints as the cosmic vision unfolds. Likewise, the novel progresses from personal trial to the tribulation of Russia, and finally to the mythic pattern of a God-bearing people who must suffer in order to redeem.

Another structural parallel surfaces in the movement through upheaval and "possession" in time, to a vision of peace and "dispossession" beyond time. Stepan has a vision at the end of the novel that is not unlike Stavrogin's in the Dresden Art Gallery. The vision comes to him on his deathbed and he tries to communicate it in his last few breaths:

> "The mere fact of the ever-present idea that there exists something infinitely more just and more happy than I am fills me through and through with tender ecstasy—and glorifies me. . . . What is far more essential for man than personal happiness is to know and to believe at every instant that there is somewhere a perfect and serene happiness for all men and for everything."[59]

Like John, Stavrogin and Stepan come finally upon a vista that opens to a cosmic renewal of creation. Only Kirillov remains closed to the possibility that the world will one day give way to a new creation, that time will be taken up into the eternal.

For Kirillov, time is a lie, an illusion which men can unmask in the supreme human act of suicide. In setting out to become the man who will liberate mankind from the illusion, he becomes the man-God who will overthrow the God-man. He chooses deliberately to rebel, to dethrone the Lamb who is the God-man crucified and risen. He not only rebels against the Lamb; he is the blasphemous parody of the Lamb who will prove the nonexistence of death and therefore the irrelevance of the crucifixion and resurrection. He is demonically possessed to the end, bestial in the refined sense of the apocalyptic myth. He personifies the beast whose head was mortally wounded (Rev. 13:3) in parody of the Lamb. He is the "false prophet" of the novel. Stavrogin asks him:

"Are you fond of children?"
"I am," answered Kirillov, though rather indifferently.
"Then you're fond of life?"
"Yes, I'm fond of life! What of it?"
"Though you've made up your mind to shoot yourself."
"What of it? Why connect it? Life's one thing and that's another. Life exists, but death doesn't at all."[60]

By killing himself, Kirillov intends to bring into existence the new man, freed from his illusion about God. This man will have asserted his freedom over against the will of God. But an unexpected dialectic emerges between the idea and its execution. In the actual execution, he is not the composed, self-possessed man who can talk with such detachment about destroying God in the calculated sting of his suicide. He is instead a man unhinged, deranged and possessed by some demonic force outside himself. Kirillov himself verbalizes the dialectic when he says, "I will assert my will, I am bound to believe that I don't believe." Ideologically, he is free, while in the act itself he is bound, possessed.

A more subtle twist in the parallel between *The Possessed* and the book of Revelation comes in the use of the word "image." Usage of this word in the book of Revelation is unique to New Testament and Christian thought. Its usual reference is to God, but in the book of Revelation it means the image of the Antichrist, the image of the devil or the image of the beast. The word *eikōn* to mean the *imago Dei* is not used once in the Apocalypse, but its use to signify the image of the Satanic beast occurs ten times (as frequently as in the rest of the New Testament taken together). In the psychic and theological realm, each of the main characters who are "possessed" in the novel carries a psychic icon of the Satanic beast and acts upon that self-image. This pattern becomes quite explicit in the discussion between Stavrogin and Tihon when Stavrogin confesses that he has been seeing a distinct image of the devil.

"And . . . and do you really see him?" Tihon asked, thereby putting aside all doubt of its plainly being no more than a false and morbid hallucination, "do you really see a definite image?"

> "It is strange that you should persist in asking me when I have already told you that I do"

is Stavrogin's reply.[61]

Kirillov's self-image is that of the man-God who will render impotent the crucifixion and resurrection of Christ, a Satanic "icon" that exacts from him the willing sacrifice of his life.

Blasphemy, deception, and idolatry run through the novel in a triadic pattern. Blasphemy is the mortal sin that will fell Stavrogin as Tihon predicts:

> "Will not your heart be filled with such hatred that you will inevitably end by blaspheming and so perish? . . . That is what I fear!"[62]

His fear is borne out. Stavrogin, like Kirillov before him, ends his life in an act of supreme blasphemy. The blasphemous word begets the violent, totally self-destructive act. It is also a word of self-deception. With Kirillov it has an ironic double twist, for Kirillov believes the rest of the world to be deceived by Christianity, and it is to expose that sham that he kills himself. Stavrogin is spiritually deceived, for he fails to see how close repentance is to forgiveness. Tihon tries desperately to convince him how near to him salvation has come because he is both hot and cold: "You have taken a great road, an unheard of road, that of inflicting upon yourself before the whole people the shameful punishment you so amply deserve." The novel is a story about deception at all levels: the psychic, social, political, and theological. Stavrogin and Kirillov are deceived by their self-images, all are deceived by the social order and by political intrigue; and theologically Kirillov is betrayed by the idea of the man-God, Stavrogin by the meaning of punishment, and Stepan by a false millennium. Kirillov and Stavrogin in differing ways idolize themselves, Pyotr makes an idol of Stavrogin, and Stepan worships the sick and doomed culture.

Satanic laughter rings in the blasphemous words and breaks out when deception is unmasked. Tihon once observes that ridicule is the world's strongest weapon; for Dostoevsky, it is the deadly weapon of the Antichrist, put into the hands of Kirillov and Stavrogin. They use it against their victims and against each other, for it has the force of a steel blade. Stavrogin's marriage to the cripple evokes from him the hellish laughter that despises social convention; his is the prototype of the sick joke. Kirillov dies with a smile that ridicules those who are dismayed at his death.

The mythic Tower of Babel rises in the imagination of the novelist to epitomize the blasphemy, self-deception, and idolatry. The image first appears in Stepan's poem described at the beginning of the novel, and overshadows all that follows. The narrator paraphrases the climactic scene:

> And finally, in the last scene we are suddenly shown the Tower of Babel, and certain athletes at last finish building it with a song of new hope, and when at length they complete the topmost pinnacle, the lord . . . takes flight in comic fashion, and man . . . at once begins a new life with new insight into things.[63]

The imagery gives shape to Pyotr's ecstatic vision of the man-God, when he finally shares it with Stavrogin. "The Pope shall be for the West, and you shall be for us!" he says to Stavrogin. "You are my idol!" he declares. "You are beautiful and proud as a God. . . . 'A new just law is to come,' and the sea will be troubled and the whole gimcrack show will fall to the ground, and then we shall consider how to build up an edifice of stone. For the first time! *We* are going to build it, we, and only we!"[64]

The myth of the Tower of Babel is the one common spring that feeds the imaginations of Stepan, Stavrogin, Kirillov, and Pyotr. It gathers up all the Babylonic pride that these figures embodied. And the Tower survives them in the rubble that bears witness to its apocalyptic fall.

West, Dostoevsky, Mann, and Lawrence have all contributed to canonizing the apocalyptic myth as a literary convention. They have demonstrated its vivifying character in monumental works of art. Each has shown the myth's claim to modernity in a different way. West deals with its relevance to the self, the self that in Lonelyhearts mirrors the soul of every man who can recognize the impalement to which his savior role is destined in a Shrike-dominated world. The mirror reflects the isolated individual fading helplessly into the dark side of the Apocalypse. The modernity of that portrait is reinforced by the post World War II fiction of Ralph Ellison and, to some extent, John Barth.

Dostoevsky broadens the focus to a whole nation, suggestive of the "nations" (*phulē*) envisioned so frequently in the book of Revelation. But his focus broadens in still another sense. The God-bearing people of Russia do not suffer fortuitously; they suffer in order to redeem. Dostoevsky's vision includes a glimpse of the light as well as dark sides of the Apocalypse. The Russian people are pictured in a process of history that is redeemable. They are the elect who must suffer in order to be truly "God-bearing." They suffer demonic possession and damnation, but do so vicariously. Unlike West's figure, the savior role in *The Possessed* can be glimpsed as a serious possibility. The suggestion, however faint, that one side of the Apocalypse can give way to the other, finds contemporary expression in Mann's *Doctor Faustus,* which anchors Dostoevsky's vision in the Western history of our time. Mann's focus is at once more precise and more universal, perhaps the most elaborate that has yet appeared in modern fiction. It is precisely this direction that the apocalyptic imagination has inspired among authors who share it: from the self, to the society, to history and its meaning.

6

APOCALYPSE OF HISTORY: *Doctor Faustus*

> *How often has this intimidating work [the* Apocalypsis*], in its urge to reveal in the language of music the most hidden things, the beast in man as well as his sublimest stirrings, incurred the reproach both of blood-boltered barbarism and of bloodless intellectuality!*
>
> —Serenus Zeitblom, in *Doctor Faustus.*

FOR THOMAS MANN'S *Doctor Faustus,* the apocalyptic myth is not only nascent in the soul and nation but is full-blown in the maturation of Western history. Mann hears the apocalyptic thunder in the bombs that ushered into our history the outbreak of World War II. The holocaust that followed was the storm that had been gathering in the heart of Western civilization, with Nazi Germany epitomizing the demonic power of that civilization.

The narrator unfolds the tragedy like a Greek chorus. He is Serenus Zeitblom, a retired professor of philosophy. Like

Stepan in *The Possessed,* he is an exile from a culture that was once stable but now is shaken to the roots by the apocalyptic tremors of his time. He provides the author with a double chronology as he alternately traces Adrian Leverkühn's life history under the Faustian curse, and chronicles the emergence and collapse of the Third Reich. The analogy of history appears incandescent in the arc of Leverkühn's career. Adrian accepts the Faustian gift of brilliance while studying at Kaisersaschern, Halle, and Leipzig. He abandons his study of theology at Halle to study music at Leipzig under Wendell Kretschmar, a Mephistopheles in the guise of a cathedral organist. As a composer, Leverkühn's truly brilliant achievements are the *Apocalypsis cum figuris* and *The Lamentation of Dr. Faustus,* each putting to music the myth for which it is named.

Midway through the novel, Zeitblom quotes a document that contains Leverkühn's hallucinated confession that he had entered into a twenty-four-year compact pledging his soul to the devil in return for an extended period of creative genius. Zeitblom later reveals that the turning point in Adrian's vocational change from theology to music was a sexual experience with a prostitute, Esmeralda, who leaves in him the venereal germ of his eventual destruction. The secret syphilis has already infected him by the time he has his interview with the devil, and the disease is symbolic of his psychic deterioration. In the mind of Adrian-Germany, it is a madness that produces the fruit of genius and then death. He finally collapses on the keyboard as he strikes the opening chords of *The Lamentation of Dr. Faustus.* He recovers from the paralytic stroke only as the demented, "burnt-out husk" of his former self. Life drains from him completely in a few brief, piteous years.

Before succumbing to the curse, Adrian grasps a glimmer of redemption in the life of Echo, his nephew. The nephew is an idyllic child, the quintessence of an unfallen creation. For Adrian, he symbolizes the new beginning, a second chance for a return to innocence. Zeitblom's description takes on mythic proportions when he describes a pastor giving Echo a colored picture of the Lamb of God after hearing the child's ethereal prayer. When Echo is stricken with cerebrospinal meningitis, Adrian's last hope vanishes before the final specter of a Satan-dominated world.

A counterpoint subplot with a further set of symbolic analogies works itself out between the violinist, Rudi Schwerdtfeger, Clarissa Rodde, and her married sister, Inez Institoris. Inez can find sexual and psychic fulfillment only through an adulterous relationship with Rudi. When Rudi finally rejects her, she follows him into a subway and shoots him. Clarissa, her sister, is an actress who is deceived into thinking she has talent. She can cope with the truth only by committing suicide. Rudi, for his part, deceives and betrays his friend Leverkühn, who is in love with Marie Godeau but cannot court her directly (symbolic of Leverkühn's isolation from the human community). He asks Rudi to propose to Marie on his behalf, but Rudi falls in love with her and woos her for himself. This whole subplot represents a sustained critique of bourgeois society. The theme is transparent in the careers of each of the characters. Each commits a form of moral suicide, a form of radical disobedience to his own nature and to the realities of life. Social critique is also historical critique of Germany, where moral suicide is apparent as a possibility in the thirties and as an irrevocable fact in the forties.

Throughout the novel, Mann makes the narrative action echo through the psychic, social, historical, and mythic realms. On the last page of the novel, it becomes evident that he has employed myth not only to enlarge the reference of the action but to redeem it. For only in the wholeness of the apocalyptic myth is there a glimpse of the redemptive miracle that Zeitblom cries for in the end. In this context, Zeitblom's closing words provide a final glimmer of grace, the hope beyond hopelessness that may redeem the catastrophe which already is set in a mythic pattern.

I. Passion and Precision

Thomas Mann has been cited as the "most violently debated figure of twentieth-century German literature,"[65] with the critical debate focused on the questionable merit of relating everything to everything else in *Doctor Faustus,* with its intricate analogy to the apocalyptic myth. The analogy is sustained, and it is as important as any in the novel. In the closing paragraph, the threads coalesce in a final tapestried image of Leverkühn-Germany plunging into the "bottomless pit" of the Apocalypse (Rev. 9:1, 2, 11; 11:7; 17:8; 20:1, 3). The image brings unmistakably to mind Leverkühn's *oeuvre,* the *Apocalypsis,* specifically the musical tableau that prefigured his descent into hell. The affinity in imagery is the author's final confirmation that the *Apocalypsis cum figuris* has overshadowed the novel as a prolepsis in music of Leverkühn-Germany. Zeitblom's long description of the composition reaches its climax by etching into our minds a Düreresque tableau: "The damned man, voluptuous in flesh, clung round, carried and drawn by grinning sons of the pit, makes horrid descent, covering one eye with his hand and with the other staring transfixed with horror into bottomless perdition."[66] In the last paragraph of the novel, Leverkühn-Germany is precisely that image: "Clung round by demons, a hand over one eye, with the other staring into horrors, down she flings from despair to despair."[67]

The analogy also appears in the use of the Faustian myth, for in discussing Adrian's shift from theology to music, the narrator has made us aware of a quasi-mythic dialectic between the divine and the diabolic. Before Schleppfuss is revealed to be a modern-day Mephistopheles, he is introduced as the incarnation of Satanic blasphemy and deception. He gives lectures at Halle that parody the Mass and ridicule the Virgin Mary. His favorite story is the tale of a maiden set upon by a Dragon who is forever marshaling converts from the Christian faith. The ludicrous but grisly story is parodically reminiscent of the dragon/woman saga in the book of Revelation: the dragon who makes war on the woman and her Christian offspring. The whole concept of the Antichrist as a Satanic figure who demonically "possesses" humans—as the tale, Schleppfuss himself, and Adrian's mythic captor all reinforce—has its roots in the book of Revelation.

R. P. Blackmur has written of *Doctor Faustus* that to work with such multilayered myth "you have to be a little solemn and dedicated, but you have also to be passionate and exact."[68] The passion and exactitude with which Mann employs the canonical myth would underscore the comment.

The Biblical literacy that Mann reveals and utilizes for his artistic purpose is no less impressive than his knowledge of the technicalities of musical composition and orchestration. Repeated mention of singing the "new song," and the "great sound," and the antiphonal woes and laments punctuate the book of Revelation.[69] The auditory symbols have an intrinsic importance for the Apocalypse that is at least as great as that of the visual symbols. Mann misses almost none of them in Zeitblom's elaborate description of Leverkühn's composition. He refers specifically to the wailing and antiphonal woes and laments, the thunder, the four voices of the altar, the voices of the four angels, the wailing of the earth dwellers, the choral response to the opening of the Seventh Seal, the "new song" of the redeemed. In the drum roll he suggests the dual sound of earthquake and thunder in Rev. 8:5; 11:19; 16:18. In what is described as "This destructive sliding through the seven positions of the instrument [trombone]!" he suggests the seven trumpets signaling destruction to mankind in various modes and phases.[70]

Mann's exactitude encompasses even the Old Testament apocalyptic sources that John drew upon. The *testis* of Leverkühn's text is taken from the visions and lamentations of Ezekiel. Zeitblom explains:

> These words, indeed, do not belong to the Revelation of St. John, they originate in another layer, the prophecy of the Babylonian exile, the visions and lamentations of

> Ezekiel, to which, moreover, the mysterious epistle from Patmos, from the time of Nero, stands in a relation of the most singular dependence. Thus the "eating of the little book," which Albrecht Dürer also boldly made the subject of one of his woodcuts, is taken almost word for word from Ezekiel, down to the detail that it (or the "roll," therein "lamentations and mourning and woe") in the mouth of the obediently eating one was as honey for sweetness. So the great whore, the woman on the beast, is quite extensively prefigured, with similar turns of phrase.[71]

Such detailed insights into the dependence of the book of Revelation upon the book of Ezekiel, together with his perception of the historical analogy in the existential situations of exile out of which both prophets wrote, reveal not merely a fertile artistic imagination, but an extraordinary degree of faithfulness to the material which he was using.

For example, first let us compare the Ezekiel passage on the eating of the scroll with that in the book of Revelation.

Ezekiel 3:1–3	*Rev. 10:8–11*
And he said to me, "Son of man, eat what is offered to you; eat this scroll, and go, speak to the house of Israel." So I opened my mouth, and he gave me the scroll to eat. And he said to me, "Son of man, eat this scroll that I give you and fill your stomach with it." Then I ate it; and it was in my mouth as sweet as honey.	Then the voice which I had heard from heaven spoke to me again, saying, "Go, take the scroll which is open in the hand of the angel who is standing on the sea and on the land." So I went to the angel and told him to give me the little scroll; and he said to me, "Take it and eat; it will be bitter to your stomach, but sweet as honey in your mouth." And I took the little scroll from the hand of the angel and ate it; it was sweet as honey in my mouth, but when I had eaten it my stomach was made bitter.

A comparison of the two passages (Ezek., ch. 3, and Rev., ch. 10) discloses that in the Ezekiel treatment the symbolism of the scroll is one of sweetness, while in the Revelation passage the symbolism is filled with paradox and irony. For there the scroll is sweet to the taste but proves to be bitter. The Dürer woodcut (Woodcut No. 11) makes it clear that the ambiguity of the Revelation passage is intended, and two different scrolls are even depicted in the woodcut.[72]

Mann gets the same kind of irony into the text of the novel through a brief expository remark about the scroll containing lamentations of mourning and woe, yet tasting sweet in the mouth of the one who eats it. His exposition is exegetically sound, based on the Revelation passage. The significance of the passage becomes evident when we see the entire novel reflected in it, so that it becomes a synecdoche of the work. An archetypal image can undergo a transformation in meaning from extreme sweetness to sweetness that has an underside of extreme bitterness as it passes from one period of history into another and from one myth into another. The whole image of Faustian man has undergone such a transformation in Mann's novel. Symbols of health and vitality represented in Luther and the Reformation are shown to have an underside that is impotent and ridiculous when reflected in Kumpf; German theological scholarship, unequalled for its rigor, slips easily and perilously into the diabolic when reflected in Schleppfuss. Music, the purest of the arts and the pride of Germany, proves to be an easy acquisition by the devil and an effective instrument in his hands. A history that was once proud for its cultural grandeur and religious vitality produces the bitter fruit of Nazism and the holocaust of World War II —the holocaust had been incipient in all that had seemed serene and healthy to Serenus Zeitblom and the *haute bourgeoisie* of Germany.[73] Adrian Leverkühn drew his genius from the drivenness of his soul, a soul tormented through a compact with the devil which was not his choice, but his fate; the brilliance of his mind proved to be the sparks thrown off by the invasion of his brain by a syphilitic disease; an artist who was cold, untouchable, abstract, and mathematical was thrust into this rarefied air through his fornication with a whore; and German history and German culture, European history and European culture, reflect the same ironical dualism, the inescapable paradox, in the imagination of Thomas Mann. The dualism, the paradox, the inevitable underside to all that flowers, the sweetness that is bitter when it reaches the stomach, reverberates through every level of analogy in the novel. Each level provides a more agonizing twist to the apocalyptic doom that has infected the brain and possessed the soul of Western man.

The novel concludes on what Blackmur calls the naked human voice, referring to Mann's own phrase. It is a cry from the heart of the narrator for *ein Wunder, das über den Glauben geht* (a miracle which will transcend, or more literally, "overflow," belief; a miracle, that is, which is more than merely spun out of the head of man-made belief). It is the miracle of apocalyptic renewal, a revelation that is the unseen, yet to be disclosed, other side of hopelessness. It will redeem the downward spiral into despair, the fall into the bottomless abyss which is the visible overturning of Zeitblom's friend and fatherland. The art, history, and culture of Western Europe, and of Western man, have come to this point in the novelist's imagination; the underside has been exposed in all its horror. But the very dualism itself—the "God-given, God-inflicted" paradox described on the second page of the novel—is also a cause for hope. The closing prayer is not a cry of despair, but of hope. It is not merely a lamentation but also a confession. For the cry lays claim to God's responsibility for the soul ("thy soul") before lamenting, "My friend, my Fatherland." The use of genitive plural instead of the normal genitive singular for "thy" reinforces Zeitblom's final appeal to a Catholic God, not a vague notion of deity, for only a Catholic would think of addressing the Godhead as *Euch*. Thomas Mann passionately raises the hope that all which has been revealed to have an ironically bitter undersiding can be turned again, or redeemed, by the very apocalyptic myth which has emerged in the narrative.

II. "The Saturation of Time and Space"

Mann's technique of sustaining an analogy to the apocalyptic myth is a special technique for telescoping time and space. In his description of the *Apocalypsis cum figuris,* Zeitblom remarks that the composition, in homage to Dürer, is intended to emphasize "the saturation of space with fantastically exact detail."[74] The linkage of early and late apocalyptic literature to the book of Revelation, the linking of the Reformation in the Dürer woodcuts to the time of the composition and to the time of the novel's narration (1946: a "postapocalyptic" time), implies a distinct telescoping of carefully selected time periods. Thus the *Apocalypsis cum figuris,* representing a saturation of space and time with exact detail, is a key analogue to the novel.

For example, the composition artistically prefigured the outbreak of the holocaust of World War II by exactly two decades: the *Apocalypsis cum figuris* was composed in 1919; Germany invaded Poland in 1939. Dürer's woodcut series artistically prefigured the upheaval of the Reformation by exactly two decades. The woodcut series, *Die Apokalypse,* was published in 1497; Luther nailed his Ninety-five Theses to the door of the Wittenberg church in 1517. The lines of temporal analogy are drawn with painstaking care, and while mathematical precision itself is often the target of parody, in this case it is more the tool of irony. It underscores Mann's preoccupation with time and history. In this multidimensional view of time and history the author moves us back and forth through the time of Ezekiel to the time of John during persecution, to the time of Dürer and Luther, to the time of the composition, World War II, and Zeitblom's post World War II perspective. He moves us along a time scale with a technique that is similar to the device used by the English novelist Virginia Woolf: varying time periods held together by the constant of a single place. Unlike Virginia Woolf, this "place" is apt to be symbolic as well as geographical. Leverkühn selects Babylon as the place of Ezekiel's writing because of its symbolism in the book of Revelation. In the imagination of the author, the Babylonian Whore infected Adrian, Germany, and Western Europe. All subsequently suffered apocalyptic destruction for their whoredom. Thus the archetypal place of Babylon is associated with Ezekiel's exile, Nero's Roman *civitas,* and Germany through the Reformation and Second World War. Music is another constant, or unifying factor, used to focus the time perspectives. The musical tableau of the composition forges a link between Jeremiah, John the Divine, Dante, Dürer's Reformation, and Germany in 1946. Thus the tableau provides a unified perspective on five periods in history, each giving successively broader focus to the others.

Zeitblom also cites the composer's achievement of a "saturation of space" in the *Apocalypsis.* The mythic "space" leading to the bottomless pit of hell is saturated with figures from Jeremiah, John, Dante, Dürer, Leverkühn himself, and Nazi Germany. Zeitblom refers to the tableau as "that crowded wall, swarming with bodies" and historic or mythic places. The musical tableau is symbolic of the tapestry that Mann is weaving throughout the novel. He moves us back and forth along a place scale from the world of Adrian's composition, to the social and psychic upheaval dramatized by the Rodde sisters, to the upheaval of World War I, and to the rupture of World War II. For example, we move through the invasion of Normandy and the robot bombs to the advancing Russian wave on the Eastern front (Chapter 33), to the description of the composition (Chapter 34), to the critique of bourgeois culture, of which the Rodde sisters are representative, back to a description of the composition, then to the suicide of Clarissa Rodde (Chapter 35).

By telescoping time and space the author creates multidimensional figures not unlike John's archetypal figures. For example, Leverkühn is a demon-possessed and damned figure from the Apocalypse; he is Faust, Germany, Babylon, artist, man. Esmeralda is at once a literal whore and the Whore of Babylon with whom Leverkühn and Nazi Germany fornicated and by whom they were infected and cursed. Echo is Adrian's nephew, but also an angelic worshiper of the Lamb, the embodiment of innocence, the "echo" of a lost paradise, a de-Satanized Kingdom of Heaven on earth; he is the beginning of a life that Adrian never knew, "the echo in infant form of the life he never lived."[75]

Doctor Faustus has been called a terminal novel. It is terminal not only as a culmination of thematic and stylistic strands that have run through all of Mann's earlier works. It is also terminal in the development of the Mann novel to the extent that plot, the sequence of events, is less important than its symbolic projection through time and space. Sequential, linear time finds its significance as it is played off against archetypal patterns; the concrete historical event must find symbolic or mythic expression—carefully and passionately—to be truly meaningful. The book of Revelation is likewise a "terminal" book, and Mann seemed acutely aware of this analogy to his art. John of Patmos wrote a vision with one eye on the historical situation facing the churches of Asia Minor and the other eye on an archetypal conflict and ultimate outcome.

III. Parody

The ornate composition which puts to music the Revelation text on the great Whore of Babylon mirrors the author's stylistic and thematic treatment of parody throughout the novel. The text is taken from the book of Revelation (ch. 17) and is quoted by Zeitblom:

> "Whore of Babylon, the Woman on the Beast, with whom the kings of the earth have committed fornication."

Only an extremely sophisticated study of the text would reveal the degree to which the element of parody has shaped John's vision of the Satanic forces. But Mann himself deals with such material with extreme sophistication. The seventeenth chapter dealing with the Whore of Babylon is the most parodic in Revelation. The florid ornamentation, which is what a coloratura musically represents, is perfectly true to the spirit of the Revelation passage describing the Whore:

> And the woman was arrayed with purple and scarlet color, and decked with gold and precious stones and pearls, having a golden cup in her hand full of abominations and impurities of her fornications. (Rev. 17:4.)

This, like all his detailed Biblical insights, is well motivated by the plot, for Adrian's study of theology at Halle could account for this detailed acquaintance with the text of the Apocalypse.

In fact, there is some question as to whether Zeitblom himself is being parodied when he evinces such surprise at the orchestration of the Revelation text, attributing it solely to Adrian's capacity for mocking imitation. To be sure, there is mockery in his imitation and the mockery extends far beyond what was intended in the primary apocalyptic myth; but the parody is executed with rigorous skill, and the selection of primary material is anything but capricious. Adrian truly has the Faustian gift of knowledge. He knows not only the Revelation text, but he knows that he, Adrian, has committed fornication with the Whore—physically, spiritually, and intellectually. In his imagination, as in the imagination of John, he understands the Whore as an instrument of the devil and the embodiment of Babylonian pride and blasphemy. Zeitblom's citation of the Revelation text, the Whore "with whom the kings of the earth have committed fornication," includes a reference to the Nazi leaders. Their *hybris* is Leverkühn's: inhuman, abstract, mathematical, detached. Like him they are infected with a crescendo of madness that is doomed to destroy them and their fatherland.

Adrian himself engages in social parody by creating dissonance in the composition to stand for "the expression of everything lofty . . . while consonance and firm tonality are reserved for the world of hell, in this context a world of banality and commonplace."[76] He also parodies the book of Revelation itself by representing the voice of John by a tenor with the voice of a eunuch who sings in a "castrato-like high register." The castrato-high eunuch represents the intrusion of the ridiculous.

We have, then, three types of parody: parody that turns on the irony of Western history and culture; parody which is the vehicle for social critique; and parody which is ridicule. These three uses of parody overlap, and the distinctions tend to be oversimplified. Zeitblom himself finds that all three merge in an exasperating way. Prompted by the ridiculous signature of Perotinus Magnus on a letter from Adrian, Zeitblom asks:

> "For a man who is not an artist the question is intriguing: how serious is the artist in what ought to be, and seems, his most pressing and earnest concern; how seriously does he take himself in it, and how much tired disillusionment, affectation, flippant sense of the ridiculous is at work? If the query were unjustified, how then could that great master of the musical theatre, at work on this his most consecrated task [the *Apocalypsis*] have mocked himself with such a title? I felt much the same at sight of Adrian's signature. . . . In short, I was consumed with loving and anxious suspicion of an aestheticism which my friend's saying: 'the antithesis of bourgeois culture is not barbarism, but collectivism,' abandoned to the most tormenting doubts."[77]

Adrian described Halle as grotesque, but it was also ridiculous, especially in the linguistic and behavioral idiosyncrasies of Ehrenfried Kumpf. Parody in all three overlapping forms permeates the entire multilayered structure of the novel's symbolism. When Kumpf speaks in the old venerated Biblical German style, Luther and the Reformation are being mocked. When he hurls a roll at the devil lurking in the corner of his study, Luther is again called to mind for his imagined scene with the devil, who appeared one day in his study. When Luther and the Reformation are being ridiculed, German culture and pride become the target critique. But as the critique moves from one level of analogy to another, all three forms are actively present in varying degrees. Mann is sufficiently in control of his parody to be comic and deadly serious at the same time. If German history is shown to have a ridiculous face on it, the face is also shown to be grotesque in the concentration camps and gas chambers. Germany's Faustian gift of knowledge and her Babylonian pride are mirrored in its art, theology, history, and culture. The parody tends to separate the author from his subject with a touch of objectivity that lends fresh credibility to what he is parodying: in this case the demon long cocooned and now loosed upon Western humanity.

The inseparability of the playful and serious sides of parody is ominous in the conversation between Leverkühn and the devil:

> I: "A man could know that and recognize freedom above and beyond all critique. He could heighten the play, by playing with forms out of which, as he well knew, life has disappeared."
>
> He: "I know, I know. Parody. It might be fun, if it were not so melancholy in its aristocratic nihilism."[78]

The supreme parody is the novelist's self-critique of his own style and technique. In writing a novel about the Faustian gift of knowledge, he has chosen a technique displaying an equally high degree of sophisticated knowledge of the Bible, of history, and of music. His obsession with technical detail leaves him open to the ironical question whether he has not constructed his own Tower of Babel. In one sense that is precisely what he has done, and he intends the ironical question to be asked. There is a twofold answer to the question of why he has done so.

One answer is that modern bourgeois man must build and climb his technically impressive Tower of Babel and fall before he can begin to hear Zeitblom's passionate prayer for redemption. This is a motif articulated in the novel: "We must again eat of the tree of knowledge in order to fall back into a condition of innocence." But Mann is not merely bent on denigrating the bourgeois mentality. He takes that modern mentality seriously, as his own technical virtuosity testifies. To the degree that Mann genuinely wants to break through to an I-Thou communication in which modern bourgeois man can participate, his critique of the bourgeois is not the one-sided critique of contempt or scorn. The technical virtuosity is parodied, but it is also a necessary process that the modern mind must go through in order to break into deeper communication.

A second answer to the question is that ridicule points, and paradoxically affirms, the object which it is ridiculing. The more deliberately parodic the devil and the demonic become, the more deeply we become conscious of the reality that is being parodied. If Echo, who is handed a colored picture of the Lamb of God, is parodied as a last hope for a de-Satanized life, we thereby become more conscious of the hope symbolized in the Echo-Lamb of God innocence figure. Surely this is what Mann meant by the hope beyond hopelessness, the transcendence of despair.

R. P. Blackmur's distinction between mockery and reversal makes the same point:

> The image of Faust as Leverkühn is not a mockery of Christ but a reversal; it works back into the conditions from which Christ is the redemption. It reminds us in its own way, and in another language, what the European Christ is for. The devil is always the other thing than God; the devil is God gone to the devil; the man possessed of the devil is the man stripped of everything human except the elementally human: those very elements out of which, after each catastrophic slump to gulf-bottom, the human can be reborn, re-made, re-created.[79]

German history did not usher in a millennium, but a diabolic reverse. By parodying the millennium, Mann can point his readers to the very reign of grace whose reverse is our history. Mann's voice is always speaking beyond Zeitblom's, echoing the mythic relief into which the narrative is thrown: "My tale is hastening to its end—like all else today. Everything rushes and presses on, the world stands in the sign of the end—at least it does for us Germans. Our 'thousand-year' history, refuted, reduced *ad absurdum*, weighed in the balance and found unblest, turns out to be a road leading nowhere, or rather into despair, an unexampled bankruptcy, a *descensus Averno* lighted by the dance of roaring flames."[80] The author does not need to weave the last threads in a mythic tapestry so nearly complete, for beyond the edge of Zeitblom's vision can be only the revelation of a new creation, an *apocalypsis* of the hope that has been a dim and aborted echo in Adrian's music —and ours.

7

THE RESURGENT MYTH IN EXILE

Fiction in this [apocalyptic] manner continues to outrun the critical absorption of it.
—R. W. B. Lewis.

THE foregoing novels illustrate the presence of the apocalyptic myth in major works of modern fiction. They illustrate how alive and contemporary it can become in the hands of an artist who knows how to give expression to the latent power of the images and symbols. Because of the stature accorded these novels by our culture, they illustrate the vitality which these archetypal symbols and this mythic language hold for the modern reader. In short, they illustrate how effectively the apocalyptic myth can break through the very language barrier that has caused the churches to banish mythic speech from their official parlance. An active, clearly discernible apocalyptic tradition is gaining momentum, and the force of the apocalyptic imagination in fiction may never have been stronger than it is today. D. H. Lawrence's *Women in Love*, Nathanael West's *Day of the Locust*, Heinrich Böll's *Billiards at Half-past Nine*, Ralph Ellison's *Invisible Man*, John Barth's *The Sot-Weed Factor*, and Thomas Pynchon's *V.: A Novel* and *The Crying of Lot 49* are important bearers of the tradition.

Through them all the apocalyptic myth exerts its force upon the twentieth-century reader, testifying to the remarkable power it can muster in its exile from the churches.

D. H. Lawrence deserves the most attention because *Women in Love* is a pivotal text. It constitutes a major break from a rationalistic plot structure, and enlists motifs and imagery from the book of Revelation as a substitute. It represents not only a radical break from the rationally ordered plot, but an equally marked departure from accepted fictional technique in characterization. The characters are meant to be representative not of real people but of primal mythic forces. It is a dancelike structure, representing the perpetual attraction and enmity of polar forces. The book revolves about the interplay between four main characters: the two sisters Ursula and Gudrun, and Birkin and Gerald, to whom the sisters are initially attracted. Gudrun is motivated by a will to possess, as is Gerald, and their mutual will-to-possession leads to a self-destructive relationship that issues in both psychic and physical death.

Birkin represents the drive toward organic wholeness, organic in the sense of cosmic as well as psychic sense, although he knows this drive is not to be fulfilled within the mechanistic, fragmented society that presently inhabits the earth. Ursula represents a dialectic between despair and desire, yielding and willing, which permits Birkin the chance to define himself and his drive within their relationship. The definition takes on mythic dimensions, which are mainly apocalyptic. A fifth character, Hermione, is important only in the first part of the novel, then disappears. She is a Satanic manipulator, bent on subjecting Birkin to her will, and she herself proves to be the reverse of all she claims to be and to want.

Gerald represents Lawrence's version of the man-God who achieves his idolatrous status, not by an act of suicide, as Dostoevsky's Kirillov does, but by imposing his will upon others. His will is projected symbolically into a larger, mythical dimension, encompassing all of civilization and the cosmos. As the industrial magnate in control of his father's mine, his will to rule the miners derives its power from the machine. His is an age of mechanization which has doomed civilization.

The apocalyptic imagery surrounding Gerald is that of a false prophet whom the "earth dwellers," in this case the colliers who work in and under the earth, worship as a "high priest." The false prophet is destroyed by the very chaos that he brings into his relationships. The destruction is ironical, for Gerald has supposed himself to be the god of order and control. Gudrun, whom he thought he had controlled absolutely through sexual domination, kills him both psychically and physically. The estrangement between himself and Gudrun symbolizes the breach between himself and the world. The destruction of organic wholeness in the real and symbolic relationship leaves him "like a victim that is torn open and given to the heavens." His death occurs before a crucifix of Christ, after falling from a summit ("always higher, always higher") of snow: "There was something standing out in the snow. . . . It was a half-buried Crucifix, a little Christ under a little sloping hood, at the top of a pole. He sheared away. Somebody was going to murder him."[81]

Gerald, too, recalls the Babylonian myth, the proud, self-exalted civilization that is utterly destroyed. Gerald's destruction personifies not only civilization's final demise but the hope of its renewal. For in the imagination of the author, planetary catastrophe presages planetary rebirth. He articulates this apocalyptic outlook in a longing for a mystic union between soul, body, and cosmos. (Birkin refuses sexual intercourse with Ursula at one point because the totality of union is not present.) Birkin says to Hermione, the Satanic manipulator bent on possessing him:

> "It is a fulfillment—the great dark knowledge you can't have in your head—the dark involuntary being. It is death to oneself—but it is the coming into being of another."
>
> "But how? How can you have knowledge not in your head?" she asked, quite unable to interpret his phrases.

> "In the blood," he answered; "when the mind and the known world is drowned in darkness—everything must go—there must be a deluge. Then you find yourself a palpable body of darkness, a demon—"[82]

Again speaking to Gerald, Birkin remarks, "Well, if mankind is destroyed, if our race is destroyed like Sodom, and there is this beautiful evening with the luminous land and trees, I am satisfied. That which informs it all is there, and can never be lost."[83] The "luminous land and trees" symbolize for him a genuinely new creation, a cosmic transformation that Birkin feels is imminent but inexplicable. Unlike Stepan and Stavrogin in *The Possessed*, Birkin has no picturesque vision of the new creation, but he reflects the novelist's conviction that prior to the rebirth, humanity must die as a consequence of its demonic will to possess. Symbolic of this death, every character in the novel is physically struck, either with a fist, a rock, or a knife, and all undergo some form of psychic suffering and death. Hermione, whose drive to possess Birkin is more intensely demonic than that of Gerald and Gudrun to possess each other, succumbs to the same psychic chaos and death that Gerald is later to undergo: "Her whole mind was a chaos, darkness breaking in upon it and herself struggling to gain control with her will, as a swimmer struggles with the swirling water."[84] But the fate of Hermione and Gerald is the exemplary fate Birkin sees for all of hate-ridden, lie-infested humanity. While he likes Gerald as a man, he despises the humanity he represents and yearns for apocalyptic judgment.

In one of the longer conversations between Birkin and Ursula, she asks: "And why is it that there is no flowering, no dignity of human life now?" To this question Birkin replies:

> "The whole idea is dead. Humanity is dry rotten, really. There are myriads of human beings hanging on the bush—and they look very nice and rosy, your healthy young men and women. But they are apples of Sodom, as a matter of fact. Dead Sea Fruit, gall-apples. It isn't true that they have any significance—their insides are full

Cross hook

man trying to save himself

> of bitter corrupt ash. . . . What people want is hate . . . hate and nothing but hate. And in the name of righteousness and love, they get it. They distill themselves with nitroglycerine, all the lot of them, out of the very love. It's the lie that kills. If we want hate, let us have it—death, murder, torture, violent destruction—let us have it; but not in the name of love. But I abhor humanity, I wish it was swept away. It could go, and there would be no absolute loss, if every human being perished tomorrow. The reality would be untouched. Nay, it would be better. The real tree of life would then be rid of the most ghastly, heavy crop of Dead Sea Fruit, the intolerable burden of myriad simulacra of people, and infinite weight of mortal lies."[85]

Birkin understands humanity's ripeness for apocalyptic judgment in terms that draw upon the apocalyptic myth in the book of Revelation. The sweetbitter imagery echoes the passage in Rev. 10:8–11 where the scroll revealing humanity to itself is sweet to the taste and bitter to the stomach. The gall apples of Sodom, rotten at the core, suggest the Rev. 11:8 passage with the dead bodies rotting in the streets "of the great city which is allegorically called Sodom and Egypt." The antithesis between the Dead Sea Fruit and the tree of life is suggestive of Rev. 22:2 which portrays "the tree of life with its twelve kinds of fruit, yielding its fruit each month."

The closest Birkin comes to a vision of the new creation is the luminous evening, the tree of life bearing new fruit, and the auditory "creative utterance":

> "The creative utterances will not cease, they will only be there. Humanity doesn't embody the utterance of the incomprehensible any more. Humanity is a dead letter. There will be a new embodiment, in a new way."[86]

Fleeting as the images are, they are suggestive of those in the book of Revelation. The luminous evening is vaguely suggestive of ch. 22:5, a vision of light without lamp or sun; the tree of life echoes ch. 22:2; and the unceasing creative utterances suggest the auditory symbols in the book of Revelation: the unceasing singing, the "new song," the thunder, the earthquake, the sound of many waters, and the harpers playing upon their harps.

While the book ends with Gerald's physical murder, that incident is "terminal" more on the symbolic than the narrative level. The destruction that Gerald's death symbolized was prefigured from the first few pages of the novel, and the mythic extension of the symbolism is what makes the novel a tour de force.

Post World War II fiction has produced a rich fare of novels that draw upon the apocalyptic myth and share Lawrence's antirationalism. In Germany, Heinrich Böll's *Billiards at Half-past Nine* follows the cursed and irrational pattern of a German family through three generations, with a conscious analogy to German history from 1907 to 1958 and to the apocalyptic myth which shadows that history. The family's struggle against Nazism is a struggle against what the novel calls "drinking from the *Host of the Beast*," and those who resist the libation are the "lambs of God." Time is compressed into a single day in the life of Robert Faehmel: September 6, 1958. The events that flow in and out of his mind that day encompass the life of his father and mother, his wife and children. His father's monumental achievement was the construction of St. Anthony's Abbey, which the son, Robert, senselessly ordered destroyed by his demolition squad during the war. The cycle of creation and destruction begins again with the grandson's decision to participate in the rebuilding of the Abbey; then at the end of the novel we see the grandfather raise his fists above a cake mold of the Abbey as though to "smash the sugared edifice to smithereens." In the assorted flashbacks that occur while Robert is playing billiards, we learn that Robert refused to make oblation to the *Host of the Beast*, and as a result was classified as one of the "lambs of God." Similarly, Hugo, the hotel clerk to whom he is telling the story, was stigmatized by his schoolmates as "God's little lamb." The language of the

Apocalypse inhabits the style and imagery of the whole book. For example, the grandfather reminisces:

> "Woe to all those who don't take the *Host of the Beast*. And of course you know that sacraments have the terrible quality of not being subject to the finite. And so they hungered, and the bread was not multiplied for them, nor the fish, and the *Host of the Lamb* did not still their hunger, while that of the Beast offered nourishment and plenty. They'd never learned how to reckon: a billion marks for a piece of candy, a horse for an apple, and then not even three pfennigs for a roll."[87]

The contrast between the *Host of the Beast* and that of the Lamb recalls the parody of the Eucharist and the imagery of the Whore riding upon the beast from whose chalice the nations drank. It recalls the beast's seductive offer of Babylonic affluence. And it suggests a parallel to the starvation wages predicted at the opening of the third seal:

> "A quart of wheat for a denarius, and three quarts of barley for a denarius." (Rev. 6:6.)

The titanic struggle of history through the two world wars of this century can be compressed on the one hand into a pattern visible in the life of the Faehmel family; but on the other hand, the dark powers at war in this struggle can be none less than the cosmic forces of the Apocalypse. Without this vision it is useless to try to understand Hitler, Nazism, or those who resisted it. What happened was archetypal, or it was nothing, nothing more than a routine game of billiards at half-past nine in the morning. But the pure pattern of billiard balls is only a balance wheel in the nearly shattered mind of Robert Faehmel, a daily balance against the chaos of a lifetime in the throes of apocalyptic catastrophe.

The American postwar fiction of Ralph Ellison, John Barth, and Thomas Pynchon differs from the German style of Thomas Mann and Heinrich Böll but is nonetheless nourished by an apocalyptic imagination. Both *Doctor Faustus* and, on a more modest scale, *Billiards at Half-past Nine* work with a clearly defined set of analogies between the history of a family, the history of Germany during the rise and fall of the Third Reich, and the apocalyptic myth which becomes incarnate in that history. The American writers tend more to a literary tradition started by Melville in *The Confidence Man,* repeated in Mark Twain's *The Mysterious Stranger,* and carried into this century by Nathanael West in *Miss Lonelyhearts* and *Day of the Locust.* It is the tradition which R. W. B. Lewis has characterized as combining the comically bizarre with the dreadfully serious, in both cases drawing upon motifs and imagery from the book of Revelation. In them all is a Satanic manipulator, sometimes visible only in other people; a victim, which may be humanity itself; and a warfare perpetrated by Satanic parody, blasphemy, and unending metamorphosis. All of them are entertainingly and forebodingly antirational, yet their purchase on truth is convincing.

Ralph Ellison is a notable example of postwar novelists who reinforce the modernity of the Westian tradition. He portrays the isolated self victimized by a Satan-dominated world. John Barth and Thomas Pynchon, on the other hand, are more concerned with the broader focus upon a nation and a civilization, thereby underscoring the modernity of the vision shared by Dostoevsky, Lawrence, and Mann. To speak of the broader scope in Barth and Pynchon is not to say that they are less indebted to West, for West's *Day of the Locust* also shows a broadening of focus from the individual to the whole society of California. When the hero of *Day of the Locust* imagines Los Angeles in flames, the apocalypse that occurs in his imagination opens upon a society, if not an entire civilization. As a group, today's novelists using the apocalyptic myth show the contemporaneity of an American tradition that began with Melville and Mark Twain and was revived by Nathanael West; at the same time they give an authentically modern stamp to the cosmic scope of a European imagination that found expression in Dostoevsky, Mann, and Lawrence.

As in *Miss Lonelyhearts,* the hero of *Invisible Man* is the victim of a fraudulent joke. The joke is the promise that he can be something other than a puppetized Negro, whose humanity is invisible to the world around him. As in West's novel, the "joke" leads him through an odyssey of violence, deceit, and suffering. And as in both of West's novels, his world explodes at the end—literally in the Harlem riot of 1943 but symbolically in a cosmic upheaval. Along his journey he meets a number of well-disguised false prophets. They are precursors of the grand dragon of deceivers, Bliss Proteus Rinehart, a Harlem minister. We never meet him directly but we meet the results of his work of seduction, bribery, and religious blasphemy. When the victim-narrator realizes that the Satanic figure has taken possession of the world and that what remains is only "an obscene swindle," he in effect acknowledges that catastrophe has come, and Satan has been loosed. The narrator's own revelation is that Rinehart "was years ahead of me and I was a fool. I must have been crazy and blind. The world in which we lived was without boundaries. A vast seething, hot world of fluidity, and Rine the rascal was at home. Perhaps *only* Rine the rascal was at home in it. It was unbelievable but perhaps only the unbelievable could be believed. Perhaps the truth was always a lie."[88] Once the author has loosed Rinehart upon Harlem and upon the mind of the hero, apocalyptic riot breaks loose—both in Harlem and in the vision of the narrator. Ras the Exhorter (for black nationalism) has become Ras the Destroyer and rides like one of the horsemen of the Apocalypse, spear in hand, through the streets of Harlem, crying for destruction and fire. From a dark pit, literally a street sewer, the hero conceives the apocalyptic pattern for the chaos, announces that he will ascend from the pit, having shed his old skin but no less invisible. Henceforth he will be a disembodied voice speaking "on the lower frequencies" for the reader.

The victim of Satanic metamorphosis and deception makes a picaresque appearance in John Barth's *The Sot-Weed Factor,* but history itself also appears on that stage. A parody on the historical novel, reviving the seventeenth-century cadences of Swift, Fielding, and Rabelais, it is a world more freighted with time than that of Ellison and West. Like the heroes in *Miss Lonelyhearts* and *Invisible Man,* Ebenezer Cooke is the target of a colossal joke. He stumbles into one ludicrous catastrophe after another. But unlike West and Ellison, Barth makes history itself the object held up for exposure and ridicule, for it is the historical novel that is equally the victim of his joke. Barth is concerned more literally both with history and with the apocalyptic myth. In the plot, Ebenezer Cooke sets out to find the New Heaven and New Earth on Maryland soil. He is commissioned by Lord Baltimore as Poet and Laureate of Maryland with the goal of writing an epic about Maryland, which he fancies will prove to be a kind of millennial paradise. The vernacular that the author has chosen permits him to refer explicitly to a bedeviled world under the power of Satan and to the book of Revelation itself: "Newton hath caught a foolish infatuation with theology, and seeks to explain the Apocalypse by application of his laws of series and fluxions."[89]

As the Apocalypse and history come thematically to the surface, so do our contemporary cultural myths. Set against the reality of the dark side of the apocalyptic myth, our cultural myths of American innocence and the sanctity of art reveal their tawdry and illusory character. The reader's laughter abates somewhat with the exposure of these myths which Ebenezer himself finally confesses: "My brave assault on Maryland—this knight errantry of Innocence and Art—sure, I see now 'twas an edifice raised not e'en on sand but on the black and vasty zephyrs of the Pit."[90] As his disillusionment with the possibility of innocence and the vocation of the artist progress, the disillusionment changes the flavor of his poem. In the end he writes not the "Marylandiad" but "The Sot-Weed Factor" (meaning "tobacco pedlar"), a bitter exposé of the entire swindle into which he has fallen.

Thomas Pynchon goes farther than any of these in the combination of apocalyptically conceived doom for our dehumanized civilization and the sick, Satanic laughter with which it shakes. Both *V.* and *The Crying of Lot 49* focus upon history directly, not as historical novels like *The Sot-Weed Factor,* but as novels whose subject is history and its apocalyptic end. At the narrative level, both are about a historical quest. At the deeper level, both pose the question of whether the revelations brought by the quest can be accepted, since they are revelations of the hideously demonic and catastrophic with which our history is charged. In *V.* a British Foreign Service man named Stencil begins a search for the identity of a mysterious woman who is represented in his father's journals by the initial "V." The mainspring of his quest is the hope against hope that the reports of her death during a World War II air raid on Malta are untrue. Were the sheer horror of the disaster to prove true, then the symbolism would suggest that the days of wrath have actually come and that history is now in an unbearably postapocalyptic stage. V. is the Whore of Babylon in modern dress. She infests all that she touches with the corruption of war, sexual perversity, and worst of all, the grotesque metamorphosis of all human life into inanition. Wherever she travels and whomever she touches, she brings with her the hoofbeats of apocalyptic terrors which herald the final Satanic curse that mankind has wished upon itself in its Babylonic perversity.

The symbolic indictment of our modern culture and world are telling and devastating. It calls to mind our whole sick preoccupation with gadgetry and our worship of inanimate things, as well as our lust for nuclear weaponry and the honor we bestow upon a technology which can provide that weaponry.

His next novel, *The Crying of Lot 49,* portrays America in a postapocalyptic stage, threatened by a dark demon from the European past, which Americans have always feared. Now America must face the question with the novel's heroine: Is the apocalyptic character of that history something to be reckoned with because it is real, or are we only a sick society suffering from paranoia? Like Barth, Pynchon uses the seventeenth century (in a Jacobean play) to be explicit about the apocalyptic theme: "Oedipa found herself after five minutes sucked into the landscape of evil Richard Wharfinger had fashioned for his 17th-century audiences, so preapocalyptic, death-wishful, sensually fatigued, unprepared, a little poignantly, for that abyss of civil war that had been waiting, cold and deep, only a few years ahead of them."[91] The heroine, Oedipa Maas, discovers through research on earlier editions of the play that a disputed line may have been a pun on "this Trystero *dies irae* (days of wrath)." An acute consciousness of the apocalyptic myth was common in the parlance and thought of the seventeenth century. But both Barth and Pynchon insist that the consciousness, if not the parlance, is no less alive in our own age. Today fear of an omnipresent "anti-God" has paralyzed our civilization. The perspective of another age informs the imaginative hold upon this age for Barth and Pynchon, as it does for Thomas Mann.

At the level of plot, Oedipa Maas has a compulsion to discover whether it is true that a demonic postal system, the Trystero, arose in Holland in 1577 in opposition to the Thurn and Taxis system and is now active in America as a diabolical plot to subvert the American system. She discovers that the Thurn and Taxis, like the whole American establishment, may have turned paranoid in fear of the Trystero and come to believe in "something very like the Scurvhamite's blind, anti-God." The demonic element in European history, from which Americans once believed themselves free and innocent, has now come upon them with a vengeance. In the face of this history they are immobilized with a dark, inadmissible terror. Oedipa herself has "revelations" that bring an intensifying, comic dread and lead to the speculation that the world has been taken over, subverted and perverted by a system of silent withdrawal: secretive but meaningless contact, hate, suicide, and sickness. The symptom and cause of the sickness is a piteously broken communication (the original Babylonic curse). Oedipa is a part of the sickness, for she too has a compulsion to find revelations in inanimate things, such as forged stamps, postmarks, and the Trystero symbol she found on a latrine wall. The sign was a muted post horn, symbolizing the gradual muting of American civilization and the symbolic reverse of the apocalyptic trumpets which herald a new word and new life.

The voices in the novel struggle at communication but they remain muted and mordant. "And the voices before and after the dead man's that had phoned at random during the darkest, slowest hours, searching ceaseless among the dial's ten million possibilities for that magical Other who would reveal herself out of the roar of relays, monotone, litanies of insult, filth, fantasy, love whose brute repetition must someday call into being the trigger for the unnamable act, the recognition, the Word."[92] The noncommunicable voices are those of American humanity, "in exile from somewhere else invisible." America has inherited Trystero's meaningless, self-destructive mechanized communication system, and that is its deadly woe, its *triste*.

The power of apocalyptic motifs and imagery is not the discovery of twentieth-century novelists. But what is so significant in the mounting importance of the apocalyptic myth in modern fiction is its ability to speak to an age which is supposed to be increasingly enthralled by rationalism. That is, the rationalistic culture of today is thought to be even more alien to myth and symbolism than it was in the day of Melville and Twain. Yet the language of the Apocalypse continues to break the barrier. Such a conscious use of symbolism and myth is now cited by many critics as one of the most hopeful trends in contemporary writing. As one critic has put it, "The most hopeful direction fiction seems to be taking at present is toward the conscious use of myth and ritual as an organizing principle."[93]

The confluence of a growing artistic commitment to supra-rationalistic forms of communication (myth and symbolism) and a growing literary tradition of the apocalyptic imagination is instructive. The literary artist does communicate to his reading public through the vehicle of the apocalyptic myth. If the great Christian myth has been exiled by the churches, it has been anything but silent or irrelevant. This phenomenon alone should bring into question some of the cherished presuppositions in the churches about the sophistication and modernity of nonmythical discourse. Culturally accommodated churches can become frozen in their choice of vehicles that relate the gospel to the modern world, just as the sectarian groups can become frozen in their choice of vehicles that preserve their cultural identity.

The widely held dictum that only nonmythical discourse can communicate with modern man needs to be reexamined on the basis of wider evidence. The churches' decision to communicate only in nonmythical form needs to be questioned on empirical grounds, as well as on the intrinsic value of much of the mythical language that churches have abandoned. Form cannot be separated from content, and the strategic or pragmatic decision to abandon the traditional form has been too hasty. Mainstream Protestant churches have a compulsion to keep up with the times in their forms of life and self-expression. That very compulsiveness can cause them to misgauge radically the spirit of our time. What appears to be proudly rationalistic may be a spirit that is as nourished by myth as any in history. The novelist's breakthrough in the face of the alleged language barrier of rationalism raises the question of how substantial that barrier really is. It raises the more important question of whether the novelist is alone in feeding a hunger which neither the culture nor the churches have acknowledged.

AFTERWORD

PROTESTANTISM today is adrift because it has misjudged the cultural climate and disowned the church's traditional language of myth. It has glimpsed the surface of rationalism but not paused to see the myths beneath. This study has attempted to show that the apocalyptic myth in particular is very much alive in the culture, or at least in that part of the culture exposed to work of the contemporary novelist. Apparently blind to this fact, the Protestant churches have abandoned the entire canonical treasure of the Apocalypse as burdensome cargo. In doing so they have abandoned the most extensive imagery of the resurrection victory that exists in the New Testament, making the cosmic drama of salvation almost inaccessible to the man in the pew. He no longer is offered a drama of epic significance in which he can participate, epic figures with which he can identify, or a cosmic picture in which he can see reality as a whole. Instead, he is asked to contribute to isolated causes in a fragmented picture of a dehumanized world.

The novelist has read our age differently. He has detected forces too immense to be reflected in any other mirror than that constructed of symbol and myth. Accordingly, he has turned to ancient, archetypal images which are the inheritance of our race and the purveyors of our Western culture. He has rejuvenated the language of myth in order to speak in an idiom that is commensurate not only with our time but with our culture. For he has detected in the culture a human isolation that will never be healed by pictures of reality in its atomistic and shapeless form; he has become increasingly wary of the "slice of life" type of narrative fiction, for life in our culture is "sliced" enough as it is. The novelist has rightly understood the modern reader's sensitivity to myth, which in its popular expression already controls and beguiles him.

It is not surprising that the majestic myth of the Apocalypse has informed and nourished the novelist's imagination. It offers a mirror that can do justice to the enormity of a darkened world, which in the suggestion of its mythic wholeness can also quicken the longing for a meaningful new day. The novelist has feasted his imagination upon the dark side of the Apocalypse: anguish in the soul, deception everywhere, and catastrophe looming over the course of human history. He invites the reader to give conscious recognition to the diabolical forces ravaging the world and resident in his own soul. It is precisely through this mythic consciousness of evil that he can come to grips with it, and with life itself. He does this in three ways. First, by admitting it to the retina of his conscious eye he can overcome the dissociation that characterizes his perception of reality; without access to an integrative myth he represses the Satanic and admits only what he can manage. Secondly, his mythic consciousness, especially as it is informed by the Apocalypse, can locate the evil in a total pattern, which calls for rebirth as well as death, re-creation as well as destruction. Thirdly, the myth gives back what so much of our civilization has taken away: the sense of brotherhood with past generations. It is a brotherhood not bound by linear time and geographical space and thus it can break the thralldom of the present moment for the lonely American who is afraid of history and deprived of what he had falsely taken to be its substitute: the frontier. As a part of this brotherhood he is in communion with those who have struggled through the centuries with essentially the same masquerade and with the same Satanic forces manipulating the masks and sowing the seeds of destruction.

Revival of the apocalyptic myth can mean nothing less than rebirth for the immobilized Christian. The Christian is immobilized in part because his church unwittingly encourages his dissociation by failing to show him a salvation drama that integrates the Satanic with the redemptive. Furthermore, if the quickening images in the book of Revelation can be restored to his consciousness, his sense of cosmic ordeal and triumph may return. His worship, witness, and discernment may take on the epic significance that it has for the apostolic witnesses to the Easter event. "Communion of the saints" may cease to be an irrelevant phrase from medieval liturgy and become instead a vivid and liberating reality. He is brother to John and to the exiles in every generation who "share . . . in Jesus the tribulation and the kingdom and the patient endurance" (Rev. 1:9). The marriage supper of the Lamb will prevail in his otherwise futile quest for communion. The image of that supper and its revelation of what brotherhood through the centuries has meant may inform his aimless search for companionship (literally, *com panis*, "with bread"). In John's circle he is one who suffers but who also conquers. The struggle is ultimate, and so is the victory in which he participates.

Once freed from the paltriness and nearsightedness that have immobilized him, he may address himself to his church's misdirected mission, based as it is upon a mistaken diagnosis of the relation between Word and culture. For until challenged, the churches will only continue to prescribe a language that neither heals nor transforms. That language, instead of sounding an Easter trumpet that can raise the dead and dying among us, could very well be tying the church to bells that toll its own quiet demise. The question of the church's language is a question of its life and death. The Jerusalemite temples can all too easily become Babylonic towers, and the failure of speech could become final.

The literary artist should be applauded for reopening the case, but the case should not be left to the expertise of the literary critic and theologian. It merits the full attention of the churches in their worship, teaching, and social action. Worship can expand the meaning of communion to include past and future generations; Christian education can unveil the grandeur of John's vision to minds enthralled by fraudulent myths; and social action, as its reference is understood to be universal as well as particular, can serve to confirm our destiny while transforming our present life and culture. Once the value of the mythic perspective is acknowledged, the church's mission can recover a dimension that is inherent in both the gospel and the modern world.

NOTES

1. The Right Rev. James A. Pike, quoted by John Cogley, "From Pulpit to Think Tank," *The New York Times Magazine,* Aug. 14, 1966, p. 16.

2. Amos N. Wilder, *The Language of the Gospel* (Harper & Row, Publishers, Inc., 1963), pp. 135, 132.

3. James A. Pike, *A New Look in Preaching* (Charles Scribner's Sons, 1961).

4. John of Damascus (eighth century), translation for a hymn by John M. Neale in 1859.

5. Wilder, *op. cit.,* p. 135.

6. Ernst Käsemann, *Zeitschrift für Theologie und Kirche,* Vol. 57 (1960), p. 180.

7. In the church school curriculum for primary, junior, junior high, and senior high departments for the year 1965–1966, there are 341 Scriptural passages recommended for use with the lesson. Of these, four references are made to the book of Revelation and not more than two or three verses in any reference. In the textbooks that pupils are asked to read at home, references to the book of Revelation comprise about .02 percent of all the passages listed, which include a total of 618 in three textbooks.

8. See James M. Gustafson, *Treasure in Earthen Vessels* (Harper & Brothers, 1961), pp. 42 ff.

9. See Reinhold Niebuhr, *Beyond Tragedy: Essays on the Christian Interpretation of History* (Scribner Library Edition, Charles Scribner's Sons, 1937), p. 44.

10. See Henry A. Kissinger, *Nuclear Weapons and Foreign Policy* (Harper & Brothers, 1957), p. 65.

11. See "The Puritan Apocalypse," an unpublished Yale doctoral dissertation (1964) by Joy Bourne, pointed out to me by R. W. B. Lewis in a conference and later in his own book, *Trials of the Word: Essays in American Literature and the Humanistic Tradition* (Yale University Press, 1965).

12. H. Richard Niebuhr, *The Kingdom of God in America* (Harper Torchbook, 1959), p. 151.

13. The Rev. Russell Conwell's classic sermon, entitled "Acres of Diamonds," earned him $8,000,000 after being delivered six thousand times.

14. F. Scott Fitzgerald, *The Stories of F. Scott Fitzgerald*, edited by Malcolm Cowley (Charles Scribner's Sons, 1951), p. 402.

15. John R. Fry, *The Immobilized Christian: A Study of His Pre-ethical Situation* (The Westminster Press, 1963).

16. *Ibid.*, p. 106.

17. *Ibid.*, p. 119.

18. *Ibid.*, p. 107.

19. *Ibid.*, p. 108.

20. See Sidney E. Mead, *The Lively Experiment* (Harper & Row, Publishers, Inc., 1963), Chapter 1.

21. Robert T. Francoeur, "For Teilhard, No Flight from Time," *Catholic World*, September, 1961, pp. 367 ff.

22. Carl G. Jung, *Psychology and Religion* (Pantheon Books, Inc., 1958), p. 736.

23. This distinction does not necessarily conform with the Greek equivalents, for in Rev. 12:1 *sēmeion*, meaning "sign," refers to an irreducible symbol.

24. Carl G. Jung, *Psychological Types*, translated by H. Godwin Baynes (Harcourt, Brace & Company, Inc., 1933), p. 616.

25. Carl G. Jung, *Contributions to Analytical Psychology* (Harcourt, Brace & Company, Inc., 1928), pp. 246 f.; quoted by Morris Philipson, *Outline of a Jungian Aesthetics* (Northwestern University Press, 1963), p. 59.

26. Carl G. Jung, *Integration of the Personality*, translated by Stanley M. Dell (Farrar & Rhinehart, Inc., 1939), p. 23.

27. Jung, *Psychological Types*, p. 560.

28. *Ibid.*

29. Jung, *Integration of the Personality*, p. 23.

30. Carl G. Jung, *Memories, Dreams, Reflections*, recorded and edited by Aniela Jaffé, translated by Richard and Clara Winston (Pantheon Books, Inc., 1963), p. 331.

31. *Ibid.*

32. *Ibid.*, p. 332.

33. See Herbert G. May, "Some Cosmic Connotations of *Mayim Rabbim,* Many Waters," *Journal of Biblical Literature,* Vol. LXXIV, Part I (March, 1955), pp. 9–21.

34. Figure is used here to mean what is more technically known as a *figura.* A *figura* is a coalescence of images of symbols having one overriding characteristic or *typos.* Thus Adam and Christ form a *figura* in Rom. 5:14, and the Virgin Mary, the New Jerusalem, and the church form a *figura* for Augustine in his *De Civitate Dei* (XVII, 16). The English word "figure" is taken from the Latin, *figura,* which would mean a general kind, nature, species, or form, especially in Ciceronian use.

35. See Jean Daniélou, S. J., *The Theology of Jewish Christianity,* translated and edited by John A. Baker (Henry Regnery Company, 1964), pp. 296–301.

36. See Paul S. Minear, "Ontology and Ecclesiology in the Apocalypse," *New Testament Studies,* Vol. 12, No. 2 (January, 1966), pp. 89–105.

37. Parody in the book of Revelation is imitation for the effect of blasphemy, usage which is more complex than dictionary definition would allow. Twentieth-century writers such as Joyce, Kafka, and Mann provide the closest parallels in contemporary writing. They first juxtapose myths, then superimpose one myth upon another. The literary critic R. P. Blackmur has drawn attention to this complex usage in a comment on Thomas Mann's *Doctor Faustus,* which is itself intended to reflect the apocalyptic myth: "Parody is something sung beside the main subject. Parody is not caricature, not satire; it is a means of treating reality so as to come short of it either on purpose or through necessity. Because it involves, points at, and limits what it parodies, parody is a good name for a means of getting at material that—in our state of belief—does not submit to the existing system. Parody is arduous, rigorous, and establishes relations in its own way. Parody points, terribly, at the reality as the devil points at God."

38. T. S. Eliot, "'Ulysses,' Order, and Myth," first appeared in *The Dial,* November, 1923.

39. Charles N. Feidelson, Jr., *Symbolism and American Literature* (Phoenix Books, The University of Chicago Press, 1953), p. 57.

40. John Crowe Ransom, quoted by Cleanth Brooks in *Modern Poetry and the Tradition* (The University of North Carolina Press, 1939), p. 46.

41. R. W. B. Lewis, *The Picaresque Saint: Representative Figures in Contemporary Fiction* (J. B. Lippincott Company, 1959), pp. 20–21.

42. D. H. Lawrence, *Selected Literary Criticism,* edited by Anthony Beal (London: Mercury Books, 1961), p. 114.
43. *Ibid.*, pp. 117–118.
44. Lewis, *Trials of the Word,* pp. 184 ff.
45. *Ibid.*, p. 235.
46. *Ibid.*, p. 212.
47. Nathanael West, *Miss Lonelyhearts and The Day of the Locust* (A New Directions Paperbook, 1962), pp. 37–38.
48. *Ibid.*, pp. 127–128.
49. *Ibid.*, pp. 42–43.
50. *Ibid.*, pp. 43–44.
51. *Ibid.*, p. 120.
52. *Ibid.*, p. 80.
53. Fyodor Dostoevsky, *The Possessed,* translated by Constance Garnett (Modern Library, Inc., 1936), p. 38.
54. *Ibid.*, p. 239.
55. *Ibid.*, p. 255.
56. *Ibid.*, pp. 663–664.
57. *Ibid.*, pp. 698–699.
58. *Ibid.*, pp. 715–716.
59. *Ibid.*, p. 674.
60. *Ibid.*, p. 239.
61. *Ibid.*, pp. 696–697.
62. *Ibid.*, p. 725.
63. *Ibid.*, pp. 6–7.
64. *Ibid.*, pp. 429–430.
65. Bernhard Blume, "Aspects of Contradiction: On Recent Criticisms of Thomas Mann," in *Thomas Mann: A Collection of Critical Essays,* edited by Henry C. Hatfield (Twentieth Century Views Series, Prentice-Hall, Inc., 1964), p. 155.
66. Thomas Mann, *Doctor Faustus: The Life of the German Composer Adrian Leverkühn as Told by a Friend,* translated by H. T. Lowe-Porter (Borzoi Book, Alfred A. Knopf, Inc., 1948), p. 358.
67. *Ibid.*, p. 510.
68. R. P. Blackmur, *Eleven Essays in the European Novel* (Harbinger Book, Harcourt, Brace and World, Inc., 1964), p. 99.
69. There is a certain ambiguity in John's use of the Greek word *legontes,* which the English translations often render only as "saying."
70. The word for "trombone" in the German text is *die Posaune,* which can mean "the trumpets of doom" as well as a trombone; it was the word Luther chose to translate the Greek word *salpigx*

(trumpet) in his translation of the book of Revelation. Thus Mann's exactitude extends to the very auditory symbols so intrinsic to the meaning of the book of Revelation. The composer is not content with a certain tonal suggestiveness; he must give musical expression to the most specific details of imagery and symbolism.

71. Mann, *op. cit.*, p. 357.

72. Albrecht Dürer, *Die Apokalypse,* Oeuvre-Katalog von J. U. Bartsch (Dresden: Verlag der Kunst, 1955), p. 14.

73. Serenus is suggestive of the German word *Serenissimus,* meaning "Serene Highness."

74. Mann, *op. cit.*, p. 357.

75. Blackmur, *op. cit.*, p. 104.

76. The reversal of dissonance and consonance extends the parody beyond Adrian's immediate world to the modern haute-bourgeoise world of banality and commonplace, of which the author is critical.

77. Mann, *op. cit.*, p. 373.

78. *Ibid.*, p. 241.

79. Blackmur, *op. cit.*, p. 115.

80. Mann, *op. cit.*, p. 452.

81. D. H. Lawrence, *Women in Love* (Modern Library, 1950), p. 540.

82. *Ibid.*, p. 47.

83. *Ibid.*, p. 65.

84. *Ibid.*, p. 118.

85. *Ibid.*, pp. 142–144.

86. *Ibid.*, p. 65.

87. Heinrich Böll, *Billiards at Half-past Nine* (McGraw-Hill Book Company, Inc., 1962), p. 143.

88. Ralph Ellison, *Invisible Man* (Signet Book, The New American Library of World Literature, Inc., 1960), p. 430.

89. John Barth, *The Sot-Weed Factor* (Universal Library, Grosset & Dunlap, Inc., 1960), p. 35.

90. *Ibid.*, p. 670.

91. Thomas Pynchon, *The Crying of Lot 49* (J. B. Lippincott Company, 1966), p. 65.

92. *Ibid.*, p. 180.

93. Stanley Hyman, *The Promised End* (The World Publishing Company, 1963), p. 348.

GENERAL INDEX

INDEX OF SCRIPTURE REFERENCES